What readers of Writer's Block Demolition think

"Having started but never managed to finish quite a few books, and having read numerous books and articles about "writers block", I was pessimistic (to say the least) about Glen's book on the subject.

I wish I'd had access to this book YEARS ago!

As an accomplished writer and project manager, Glen doesn't fill your head with nonsensical ways to avoid (or just put up with) writers block. Instead, he dissects the actual process of writing a book and, with carefully thought-out exercises, gets you to work your way through it from start to finish. He delves into the emotional connection and describes models of motivation, showing you how to increase your desire to write, how to decrease the effort involved and how to link these to methods for increasing the time you have available and using that time more effectively.

Each stage of dissection is filled with real-life examples, which means that you'll understand them immediately, instead of having to wonder what was meant.

The entire book flows as a well-executed plan, with the desired result being the realisation of your goal; to write that book!"

– Tony Ross, Ross Software Solutions, Scottish Highlands, UK
   http://www.RossSoftwareSolutions.com

presents

WRITER'S BLOCK DEMOLITION:
Finding the Time to Write, Keeping Writing, and Finish Your Book

**By
Glen Ford**

Published By
Training NOW
Mississauga, Canada

Sale of this book without a cover may be unauthorized. If this book is without a cover, it may have been reported as unsold and destroyed. Neither the publisher nor the author will have been paid for their efforts.

© 2012, Glen Ford and TrainingNOW

All rights reserved. No part of this book may be reproduced in any form or by any means without written permission from the publisher. If purchased in electronic form, the purchaser may make a reasonable number of copies for personal use as backup or to view on alternative media. The creation of copies for lending or resale is forbidden.

Published by TrainingNOW, Mississauga & Oakville, Ontario, Canada
http://www.TrainingNOW.ca
http://www.LearningCreators.com

ISBN (Kindle Edition):   978-0-9917762-0-7
ISBN (Print Edition) :   978-0-9867885-9-8

Limit of Liability/Disclaimer of Warranty: While the publisher and author have used their best efforts in preparing this book, they make no representations or warranties with respect to the accuracy or completeness of the contents of this book and specifically disclaim any warranties of merchantability or fitness for a particular purpose. No warranty may be created or extended by sales representatives or written sales materials. The advice and strategies contained herein may not be suitable for your situation. You should consult with a professional where appropriate. Neither the publisher nor author shall be liable for any loss or any other commercial damages, including but not limited to special, incidental, consequential or other damages.

This book is dedicated to my readers
who give me a reason
to write
And to my family
who make it all worthwhile

Acknowledgements

How do you thank everyone who participates in any book of this type. From the editors who complain about my style to the family that complains about my spending so much time and effort on the book. From the early readers and the reviewers (who really should complain) to the many writers who have commented on this subject long before I did.

All I can say is "Thank you". (And to my wife ... "I really do want to pay attention to you — you just have to get my attention first!")

And then of course, there is you the reader. Who really should be thanked because without you there is no reason for me to do this writing thing. Without your attention (and yes, pennies and dimes) I couldn't afford to do this at all. I can only hope that my opinions help you in the end. And that someday, I will be reading your books.

TrainingNOW Books By Glen Ford

How to Write Your Own How-To EBook in 24 Hours or Less: The Information Products Secret Revealed!

How to Document a Project Plan: What You Need To Know To Design A Project Management Plan Quickly and Easily

How to Blog for Money: 9 Strategies to Get Your Blog Earning Money Online and Off

As Glen Douglas

How To Build A Raised Garden Bed

With Paul Benson

101 Limericks About Public Speaking

Contents

1. THE ETERNAL ENEMY	**1**
WHAT DOES IT TAKE TO BE A WRITER?	1
WHO AM I AND HOW DID I LEARN THESE TECHNIQUES?	6
THE "AGENDA"	11
2. THE WORK EQUATION	**17**
THE "WORK EQUATION"	17
THE SOLUTION	22
3. HARNESSING THE FORCE THAT OVERCOMES	**25**
CREATING THE DESIRE TO WRITE	25
WHY MOTIVATE?	28
MODELS OF MOTIVATION	32
MASLOW'S "HIERARCHY OF NEEDS"	35
"TIME AND MOTIVATION" MODEL	40
"EMOTIONAL INERTIA"	43
THE "BIG THREE MOTIVATORS"	46
FIGURE IT OUT FIRST	51
HOT BUTTONS AND COLD SHOWERS	57
FOUR TRICKS	58
TRICK #1: YOU CAN'T FORGET	61
TRICK #2: SELF-INFLICTED PATS	63
TRICK #3: CREATING A CRYSTAL BALL	67
YOUR ASSIGNMENT IF YOU CHOOSE TO ACCEPT IT	71
4. MAKING WRITING EASIER	**73**
THE POWER OF SYSTEMS	73
WHY IS YOUR SYSTEM = YOUR SUCCESS?	78
WHAT TO LOOK FOR	88

EXAMPLE OF A WRITING SYSTEM	**96**
PROCESS DECOMPOSITION	97
DETAILED DESCRIPTION OF ELEMENTS	98
RECOGNITION OF DIFFERENT VARIATIONS OF TASKS	98
ISOLATION OF DIFFERENT TYPES OF THINKING	100
USE OF COGNITIVE TOOLS	101
APPROPRIATE LEVEL OF DETAIL	101
BUILDS IN CONSISTENT QUALITY	102

5. FINDING YOUR OWN WRITING HOLE — 105

SYSTEMS ARE MORE THAN JUST PROCESS	105
WHAT IS A WRITING HOLE?	106
WHY HAVE A WRITING HOLE?	108
WHAT TO LOOK FOR IN A WRITING HOLE	110
CONTROLLABLE	110
AVAILABLE	113
PRIVATE	115
SPACIOUS	117
SOMETIMES I NEED	118
FINDING YOUR WRITING HOLE	120

6. IT'S ALL IN THE WRIST — 127

THE THIRD OF THREE	127
THE **YOU** IN THE SYSTEM	128
WORK HABITS	132
BE KIND TO YOUR BODY	133
TAKE BREAKS (NOT JUST SLEEP)	140
CREATE WRITING RITUALS	142

7. TURNING OFF WRITERS BLOCK — 145

THE THREE CAUSES OF WRITER'S BLOCK	145
THE THIRD FACTOR	148
ONE WAY TO CATCH THE RABBIT	150

8. DEFEATING THE THIEVES OF TIME — 155
FINDING THE TIME — 155
WHY WE LOSE TIME — 156
REDUCING AVOIDANCE — 158
ELIMINATE THE TIME GOBBLERS — 161
GET AROUND CONFLICTS — 165
   SCHEDULE YOUR WRITING TIME. — 166
   SCHEDULE YOUR DAY — 167
   THREE STRATEGIES FOR STEALING TIME — 168

9. CONCLUSION - TIME TO GET STARTED WRITING — 175
10. ABOUT THE AUTHOR: — 178

"Twenty years from now you will be more disappointed by the things that you didn't do than by the ones you did do. So throw off the bowlines. Sail away from the safe harbor. Catch the trade winds in your sails. Explore. Dream. Discover."
- Mark Twain (Samuel Clements)

Chapter 1:

The Eternal Enemy

What does it take to be a writer?

The blank page.

The first word.

The terror of the initial idea.

I don't know of any writer who likes to stare at that terrifying eye into the soul. Nevertheless, each of us does it. We stare into the depths and pray that a word — any word, never mind the right word — suddenly appears. Or better still that 250 words suddenly sprinkle the empty page's frightening surface.

Every writer has suffered from the SBWBNRN syndrome. That's the "Should Be Writing But Not Right Now" syndrome for those of us that don't speak in acronyms. You know the set of excuses that starts "I want to write but I can't seem to find the time!" or "I keep trying to write but something else keeps getting in the way!" and invariably results in that empty sheet sitting in the typewriter. Yes, I know that most writers use PCs, or Macs, or tablets, and that the typewriter is an anachronism, but work with me here. The remnants of the past are more powerful than the dreams of the future. Especially when it comes to not having written.

Speaking of the past, do you remember the "Perry Mason" TV shows with Raymond Burr taking charge of the courtroom, slicing through to the truth (and always proving his client's innocence)? Did you ever wonder where those stories came from?

A gentleman by the name of Erle Stanley Gardner wrote them. Mr. Gardner was a mostly self-taught lawyer who spent twenty years practicing law in California. He loved trial work and defending the poor. Unlike most modern lawyers, his clients were mostly poor agricultural workers who were lucky to pay him with a scrawny chicken. He barely made a living. In fact, he wrote books at night to help put food on the table.

Initially they were just "pulp fiction" and not particularly successful. After all, have you ever heard of A.A. Fair, Kyle Corning, Charles M. Green, Carleton Kendrake, Charles J. Kenny, Les Tillray and Robert Parr? However, when he wrote about what he knew and loved — the law and the fight in the courthouse to establish guilt or innocence — they became something bigger. Something that touched both his heart, and the heart and wallets of his readers.

Erle Stanley Gardner set a writing goal of 66,000 words a week. In the days of retyping the whole page to make a minor revision, he set a goal of writing a 264-page book per week. He determined this figure from the advice of William Wallace Cook, a successful pulp writer whose work Gardner admired. In time, Erle Stanley Gardner, wrote over 80 *Perry Mason* books, and eventually gave up his law practice to write fulltime.

Now it may seem that this is a story about someone becoming successful by writing about his or her passion. And it certainly can be used for that purpose. In fact, it usually is. But there is more than just passion to this story. There is a lesson for those of us who wish to find the time to write.

Remember that Gardner was a full-time lawyer. He spent the usual 60 plus hours working in his practice. But he still found the time to write. He made writing a priority. He squeezed the time to write out of the little time he had available to eat, sleep, and relax. In fact, he set a goal that most full-time writers would have a problem achieving. And as a result, made his mark on the world. That mark has lasted over 80 years. It has included movies, television, and books.

Now, I'm not suggesting for a moment that you can find the time to write the 66,000 words a week that Gardner's mentor, William Wallace Cook, suggested in his 1912 book, The Fiction Factory. In fact, I don't finish that many words in a week working full time. However, if Erle Stanley Gardner can follow this advice in his spare time, then surely you can find the time to write to your personal goals.

People are interested in writers. Tell them that you write and they'll ask you "what do you write about?" and "Where can I read some of your work?" If you're a real writer, the answers are easy.

"I write about what I am passionate about."

"Right now I am writing a ... about..., and I'll have it finished by... "

"You can find my work at... and ..."

"And then I am going to write about ... (whatever your next project is)"

If you are not a real writer, but you just like the attention, then your answers to the same questions are more along the lines of:

"Well I have two chapters of my novel done, but then... happened..."

"I also started..."

"I will get back to it as soon as..."

"I am hoping to get some articles published by..."

See the difference?

There are only two certainties in life ... and it's not death and taxes. The first is that everything ends and the second is that if you don't start you'll never succeed. You can be deliberate and intentional with the ending. And you can guarantee failure by never starting.

Writer's Block Demolition

Who am I and how did I learn these techniques?

I am a writer — I've always been a writer. I've been writing since I was knee-high to a grasshopper. I remember handing in a creative writing essay in Grade 8. It was over 30 legal sized pages long — in my almost illegible scrawl. In fact, the teacher's comment was that a couple more assignments like that and I'd have a novel. (At the time, novels averaged about 150 to 200 pages).

However, I've had this problem for the longest time — making the time to write. After all, I have a professional career outside of writing — and a family. I'm running several businesses and finding time is a problem. Time for anything is a problem. Including sleeping and eating — ask my wife. She used to turn off the light to get me to go to bed. Then she realized I would just keep working in the dark. Finding the time to write kept me from fulfilling my writing potential - and it drove me crazy!

You see, I have to create and if I don't create ... well, I start going a little strange. People think I'm a little strange to start with. So going stranger ... well, you can fill in the rest.

In my other life, I'm a project management consultant. That means I am an organizer, an analyzer, and a planner. In a word, I'm a problem solver who gets things done. As a project manager, I manage complex projects where things absolutely must get done (and done well) on a precise schedule, with no excuses accepted.

I also have a growing family — so finding time for family activities is even more important to me. I love my family and I don't want to be one of those fathers that missed them growing up. My luck in life has caused enough of that. I'd hate to wake up one morning and have a six-foot son. (Too late! Even my youngest is taller than I am.)

In short, I don't have time for the luxury of writer's block or the problem of finding the time for writing. At least, not if I'm going to get any personal writing done.

But of course, I do suffer from those problems like any other writer. As a result, I needed to figure out what was really going on with my writing, and then fix it. Of course, I couldn't create more time. Instead, I finally discovered how to make the best use of the time I have.

So how did I end up creating this series to share my discoveries with you? First a bit more background on how I ended up writing books like this one.

Writer's Block Demolition

When my business partner and I set up TrainingNOW, we needed to find the best ways of working and providing exceptional training. We have lots of experience — between us, about 50 years. That's more than enough experience to build the skills our training is based on. All we needed was to make that count.

You see, I am disabled. Nothing that stops me working, but I walk with difficulty and I use a cane. My business partner is in the same boat — only worse — and both of our wives have challenges as well!

As a result, well, we had a problem. Giving live ("face-to-face") training sessions is difficult. I used to do a lot of it, but now standing for an extended period doesn't work for me, and sitting isn't much better. And for Paul, well, he's in even worse shape. I just suffer — he can't leave his wheelchair. If we were going to do double team training, we would always have to hire someone to help. The best solution for Paul, myself, and our company was to switch our efforts to specialize in training over the internet. That's where LearningCreators came from. But then, of course, we started encountering some of the problems from that decision.

One of the first challenges we encountered, was how to write eBooks quickly. When we first started, we were told, "You need to write eBooks and sell them." Now both of us have written books before for other people. We know exactly how much work is involved. It just wasn't going to be practical using traditional methods.

We had to figure out how to write self-help eBooks quickly.

Those eBooks still had to provide high-value, reliable and practical advice that our readers could use to improve their own professional activities or to expand confidently into new areas. We didn't want to become known for churning out poor quality garbage. And quality takes time. So we had a major dilemma.

Then I realized that our customized training methodology — how we create high-quality training courses quickly and consistently — could be adapted to help with the writing challenges. This breakthrough addressed one of the major problems writers face — that writing is hard (or appears to be). With a robust and reliable writing system, it doesn't have to be such a chore.

Of course, then I needed to simplify the system and deal with issues that others would encounter with the system. Nevertheless, I had the base. All it took was to test the solution and voila, our book "How to write your How-to Book in 24 hours or less" was born.

Okay, good commercial so far. So why am I going into this?

Once I solved the problem of writing a quality book quickly, I started to find the other problems that other writers encounter during their normal writing lives. After all, I was cranking out books — or was supposed to be cranking out books — the same way they did.

But getting that next book done was a lot more difficult than I thought it should be. Especially since the actual writing process was dead easy.

The biggest problem I found was just getting started. Writers seem to love having written but they hate the act of writing. Most writers seem to have a problem just getting going. And I'm no different. We even have a name for one form of it — WRITER'S BLOCK. The fear of the blank page!

So naturally, I went to the experts to learn how to get over my writer's block and time problems. There were ideas and ideas and ideas. But no solutions. It seemed like everyone had part of the solution. Everyone focused on something that interested him or her. Maybe it was finding minutes here and there. Maybe it was creating the perfect office. But it seemed that no one could agree on how to solve the problem.

Of course, I'm a problem solver by profession and by nature. And I don't believe in dealing with problems more than once. Being a project manager has taught me to look for holistic solutions to problems. So I worked to create a systematic method of solving writer's block. Something that would always work (or almost always) and could be easily understood and implemented. I began at the beginning and worked my way to the end, avoiding falling in love with any particular piece of the puzzle. This book grew out of that research and my efforts to solve writer's block, time management, and related problems. And of course, from how I've solved those problems for myself.

And the frightening thing is — it's really very simple.

The "Agenda"

This book is designed to help writers who are having trouble finding time to write.

But it's also designed for writers who didn't manage to get the writing done when they *did* have the time.

And it's for writers who thought they couldn't get the writing done — because it's just too hard, and there's always something else to do.

And of course, it's also designed for writers who are tired of staring at the blank page. No, I haven't forgotten you. And yes, we will solve the writer's block problem. In fact, we have to. It's part of the whole time to write problem. But first, we need to get you sitting down and writing. So we're going to talk about that first.

At one time or another, I have had all of these problems. Instead of giving up, or accepting so-so results, I decided to find out what was the real issue — and fix it. It turns out there are a bunch of issues and they all need to be addressed if you are going to write at your full potential.

In this book, I'll identify the *real* problems that prevent you from writing. You'll also discover (at least) two sets of good news: First, that it's not your fault. It's not that you're lazy. Some very specific roadblocks are stopping you. And second — and most importantly — that all of these apparent roadblocks are totally fixable.

In the process, I'll give you practical, proven solutions that will get you past those problems that are holding you back. Once you've eliminated them, you'll be able to zoom along and enjoy the thrills of writing.

Let's get something out on the table right now. Writing should be fun *not* drudgery. When you are "in the flow", expressing yourself in words is almost as good as ... (Well, you supply the comparison)! It's a high as good as any drug. And it's a high we share with any other creative pursuit. We deserve that high. We've earned it. That high is not something that should be lost to the one-eyed monster that is the blank page. There is no reason we should accept anything less than this.

To help you get writing back on track, I've broken this book into four major sections.

Chapter 2 discusses the Work Equation. This model will show you the key points you need to consider in order to solve your "lack of time" problem and jump-start your writing. This key chapter will provide you with an overview of what causes problems with finding the time to write. Hopefully, when you finish you will already be beginning to identify where your biggest problems lie.

In Chapter 3, I'll show you how to harness the force that overcomes all obstacles. We're going to show you how to build a force within you that will allow you to blow down the walls that are preventing you from writing. And no, this isn't a feel good, new age, mind control sort of thing. It's just old-fashioned people management turned inward. It was tried and proven when my father was managing people. It was tried and proven when my grandfather was managing people — even if he never used it. It has been tried and proven throughout my management career. And it works whether you're Gen X, Gen Y, or Gen old and crotchety.

In Chapter 4, 5 and 6, I'll focus on making writing easier. I'll show you the power of having a writing "system". And I'll show you what you need to have in your own writing system. I also won't forget to include the unspoken part of a system. I'll give you some hints for finding a place to write. And I'll give you some hints on how to set up your own "writing hole". I'll go on to talk about your work habits and how they affect your writing.

Finally, in Chapters 7 and 8, I'll wrap show you how to eliminate the last, sad remnants of the problems. In Chapter 7, I'll show you how to find ideas and eliminate the last source of writer's block. And in Chapter 8, I'll show you how to find the time to write when you don't have any time. This is the part that seems at first glance to be the whole solution — but isn't. More importantly, I'll show you how to bring it all together to defeat the "Thieves of Time" and ensure that your writing experience is the best it can be.

At the end of this book, you'll know:

- The three elements that prevent you from actually sitting down and writing

- How to motivate yourself so you don't stop writing
- How to make your writing easier — so you don't fear it
- Ten ways to find the time to write (and still have a life!)
- How to be sure you'll never have writer's block

Now let me introduce you to what I discovered in my own journey and to the complete series of steps that will have you writing like never before!

"The artist is nothing without the gift, but the gift is nothing without work"
*- **Emile Zola (1840-1902) French artist and philosopher***

Chapter 2:

The Work Equation

The "Work Equation"

Okay so I had to fight with my busy lifestyle to find the time to write. And that forced me to figure out what causes writer's block and getting around the black hole that sucks up all of a modern writer's time. So what did I find out?

I summarize my personal learning in what I called the "Work Equation".

Right about now, you may be saying to yourself "Uh Oh! — This sounds like theory. I was never good at math or science in school." Or worse, "I can barely add and subtract and he wants me to do higher math?"

Don't worry this isn't theory! This book is totally focused on giving you a set of practical approaches to solving your time and organization problems, and for getting you writing effectively and consistently. And of course, eliminating writer's block.

The "work equation" is not a piece of scientific theory — it's just a model. Models describe observations about a problem. They usually do so by describing how the related forces interact. In this case, the model describes a set of problems that, at first glance, seem to be just one problem — finding time to write. The easy way to describe a set of problems and how they relate is to use an equation. Of course, my mathematics professors would have dismissed it as unworthy of being termed an equation but we call it an equation nonetheless. After all, we have to call it something. (Actually, strictly speaking, it's called a function — but I'm a writer not a mathematician so I really don't care!)

So let's start with the problem of not having the time to write. After all, if you can't find the time to write it doesn't much matter if you have writer's block. In effect, we'll address writer's block as a particular form of not having the time to write.

Remember my mentioning the research I did on the problems of writing? Well it turns out that there are three important components to not having the time to write, not just one. If you don't specifically address all three, you won't get the results you're looking for.

All three elements that control your writing have to align if you are going to be a real writer.

The "Work Equation" says that the amount of writing done is a function of the desire to write less the effort to write, and the time to write. (For the mathematicians in the audience Writing= $f[(\text{desire} - \text{effort}) \times \text{time}]$). The actual model is a little more complex. It takes into account such things as your speed of writing and so on. However, for our purposes all we need to deal with are the core factors — desire, effort, and time. Using these criteria, no writing work will occur *unless* the desire to write and the time available, in combination, are greater than the effort involved in writing.

If you don't have the **Desire** to write - and you can't motivate yourself, then you will only ever end up with a bunch of partially complete pieces. An incomplete article or two, a couple of chapters of that great first novel, the outline for the definitive work on... and so on until your disk drive is filled with drek. And someone calls you on your claim to being a writer.

But being motivated isn't enough on its own. You must focus that desire into action. Desire without action is simply dreaming.

The second part of the game is **Effort**. If desire is the car and the motor, effort is the trailer it is towing. The writing project you are tackling must appear to you to be manageable. You may already know how big a writing project you can take on, and complete successfully. Or you may be finding every individual writing project you come up with to be totally overwhelming. That perception is based on some form of reality. It takes work to write. If the effort is too large, you will never start to write because you will be too frightened to begin.

Regardless of whether you have a number of successful writing experiences behind you or not, the actual work effort involved in writing can be reduced by using a "writing system" that streamlines how you do the work. We'll learn later that it's also a key element to eliminating writer's block.

You may already have developed your own informal system for how you write. You might even have developed a formal system. Writing without having any writing system will always result in problems and make the work harder than it needs to be. That's why it's always harder to write your first novel than your tenth. Even if you don't have a formal writing system when you start, by your tenth book you'll have developed an informal system at the very least.

Finally, you have to have the ***Time***. If you don't have *any* time available then you absolutely can't write. Writing is work and work takes time. It doesn't just magically appear. No matter how much we might want it to. On the other hand, most of us have *some* time available that we could allocate to writing. We just don't. Instead, we use it elsewhere.

Even when we have *lots* of time, we still don't get the writing done. We're always going "to do that next", or "when I get around to it", or "well there's no rush ..." Without setting priorities and focusing on actually sitting and writing, nothing ever really gets started. So nothing ever gets done. Finding the time to write will always include focusing on writing as a minimum.

Making matters worse, you can't just write for short periods, on those odd occasions when you feel the urge. You need to be writing consistently, professionally, and to a high quality. That's how you steadily build your reputation. That's how you are going to build your skill. Writing plus reading equals more skill. No writing (or no reading) means no skill. You have to allocate time for both. Then you need to sit and do both activities.

You may be feeling "But writing every day won't work for me. And it will be too much effort ..." That's why this book and the video it grew from are so important. You don't have to feel this way. By the end of this book, you'll know how to work better, easier, and just how much you can accomplish. You'll find the missing links that are currently preventing you from writing. And you'll be surprised, when you fill in those missing links, to find yourself rushing to start your next writing project!

The solution

So now, we know where the problem is. How do we fix it? How do we find the time to write?

The "Work Equation" is the starting point for you to build a sound "practice of writing". Regardless of the type of writing you do, this "equation" gives you the insight you need to increase the amount of writing you do.

The amount of writing you produce will increase when:

- you increase your desire to write
- you decrease the effort involved
- you increase the time available AND you use that extra time effectively

It's simple. The more you want to write. The more likely you are going to write. And the more likely you are going to continue writing. So we need to increase you real desire to write. Not the dream. Not the wish. The desire. The passion for writing. How do we increase your desire to write? That's no secret. It's called motivation. It's what managers have done for years. But unlike the motivation you've encountered at work — this is self-motivation. It's basically the same thing. It's just a little simpler to do and a little less fraught with error. It's focused on you not the person next to you. So since you can usually read your own mind (which isn't something most people can do with others), you can tailor the techniques to work effectively for yourself.

The second piece of the puzzle comes when you decrease the effort involved. Cool. The solution to that isn't unknown either. It's called a writing system. A writing system's whole purpose is to make it easier to write. Now, I want to be clear about something. There's a reason it's called a system not a process. There's more to a system than just a set of different tasks. I'm not going to get into a battle of terminology here, but a system includes the actors, and the environment that you are performing in, as well as the process itself. So it's far more than just do this, do that. And then discovering you've been doing it to the wrong things or using the wrong tools to do it with.

Finally you'll increase your writing when you increase the time available AND use that extra time effectively. Of course, that can be the most difficult element. It's what most time management systems think they need to focus on. And it's what you may believe to be the real problem. But as I've said, it is only part of the problem (and in fact, the least part).

Welcome to the modern world. We're all short of time. We've all got full schedules. We're all faced with "Time Grabbers". Those "Time Bandits" that steal our minutes and hours. And yet, despite these time gobblers, some of us find the minutes to produce books. You need to reduce the power you've given to these thieves and then steal back some of the time that you have lost to them.

From the interactions of the three criteria in the "formula", you can see how addressing each of these areas will give you new insights, and new tools to get the best results with your writing activities. However, you should also be able to see how addressing only one part (say desire or time availability) while ignoring the other two will ultimately fail. This is why most time management 'systems' fail to help you find the time. They address only the time part of the problem without addressing the other two causes.

"You must stay drunk on writing so reality cannot destroy you."
— **Ray Bradbury, Zen in the Art of Writing**

"Writing a book is a horrible, exhausting struggle, like a long bout with some painful illness. One would never undertake such a thing if one were not driven on by some demon whom one can neither resist nor understand."
— **George Orwell**

Chapter 3:

Harnessing the Force that Overcomes

Creating the desire to write

In this chapter, I will specifically address the issues involved in desire and motivation. I'll show you how you can get yourself "pumped up" to write. Don't underestimate the importance of motivation. Or overestimate your own current motivation. The title of this chapter "Harnessing the force that overcomes" all obstacles, is a recognition of how powerful your need — your will — to write can become. And how powerfully it can affect your writing output.

Your desire to write is the one force that really can overcome all obstacles. It is the one force that can make writing not only fun, but a "must do". It can drive you to find the time when there doesn't seem to be any time available. That's what making time is all about.

Too often, writing is just work. Not fun. Not easy. Some people might even call it drudgery! That's when the problems start. It's why most writers don't like writing. It's silly. We're writers. It's our calling. It's the basis of our jobs. It's the driving force in our life. And yet, as much as we love having written, we hate the process of writing.

Part of the reason we don't like it is we don't have the desire to write. We all go through those bouts. If you have the desire to write, it's fun to write. It's something you want to do. It's something that you love doing. It will even overcome a poor writing system.

Without desire, you don't want to tackle writing. You will find a million things that need to be done first. "I have to sort my ties." "I can't write with a messy desk! I just can't think with this mess." The excuses are endless. Hey, if anybody sees my desk — trust me you can write with a messy desk.

In Stephen King's book "On Writing", he tells the story of the enormous desk he just had to have so that his writing would go better. Until he had that desk, he couldn't really achieve his best. That desk was his cure-all, his "silver bullet." So he finally got the desk. And nothing changed. You see, he discovered it was something in him that was needed — not a change of furniture. And that insight allowed him to solve the real problem. Eventually he rediscovered his passion for writing, the barriers preventing him from writing all disappeared, and the rest is history.

Being motivated is a key requirement for you to get your writing projects accomplished. Otherwise your garage gets organized, the cat gets a bath, the tea gets made, the coffee gets made, the floor gets cleaned, the dishes get washed, the mail gets walked to the corner. But as far as new writing is concerned? Well, let's just say that no new writing appears magically on your computer screen, placed there by small magical writer's leprechauns. Only shoemakers are that lucky!

So in this chapter I'm going to focus on:

- Why you need to motivate yourself (and not just sit back and dream about writing…)
- What is this "motivation" thing
- What are "models" and why they are different from theory
- A look at some well-known models of motivation
- Using models to understand and predict real world results
- What you need to do to motivate yourself
- Why motivation is personal and why what motivates me won't necessarily work for you
- And then I'm going to give you three tricks to motivating yourself and three specific methods to consider

Why motivate?

Why do we need motivation? Either for ourselves or for others?

We usually motivate for one or both of the following reasons:

- To activate desire

Harnessing the Force

- To focus desire on a certain activity and/or outcome

Let's suppose that you are coaching a local little league baseball team, then the first thing you want your players to concentrate on is the feeling they get from playing the game as members of a team. You have to tell them how special that feeling will be. When the team scores a home run, or strikes out a batter — when everyone cheers and high-fives each other — that is the experience you are inviting them to share.

When you've fired them up so that they yearn to play with the team, then they just can't stand to miss a game. It is unlikely they will get bored and stare off into space. More likely, they will savor every minute they are out on the field, or eating hot dogs with their teammates!

You've activated their desire to play.

At that point, they may not know too much about the rules of the game. They may run into each other from time to time when catching in the outfield. I've seen them hit each other with the bats. I mean, it can get a little dangerous out there. You're going to spend a lot of time just preventing the most severe injuries. But, you can guarantee, they will be playing their hearts out for the team and that feeling of being included, of being special.

In time, they'll meet tough, more skillful teams. They might suffer losses that affect morale. At that point your job changes. As the coach, you need to focus them on what is important — building skills, gaining experience to use in future games, looking for opportunities for that breakthrough win. You have to focus them on playing as a team.

You work until their motivation focuses on playing well. The game and the team are still big incentives to play, but they are seeking more: a first win, a top ten position in the league, making it to the regional championships...

It's corny but true. There are obstacles to every human endeavor. Someone with strong motivation can overcome these challenges, one by one. You can't overcome all of the challenges at once. It can't be done. It's disheartening to try. But each challenge met and overcome, each new accomplishment reinforces the feeling of confidence in your abilities. And moves you one step further to achieving them all.

But what happens if motivation can't be achieved for whatever reason? Unmotivated players typically don't turn up for practices. For lots of little reasons, of course: too busy with other things, time conflicts appear, they feel sick, they're too tired, they forgot. They give up when they encounter their first difficulty — tired legs from running after hits, coordination issues, getting hit by a ball... the list is unending. But the result is always the same.

A low level of motivation might get you past a few small obstacles, but as time goes on and the challenges get harder, that small desire to succeed may prove inadequate. In our baseball example, after the sixth straight loss half the team might say, "That was a waste of time" or "I never liked playing for this team anyway". They may quit or start missing practices. In fact, they might never play again.

So you're really motivated. So what? Most times, being motivated is still not enough on its own. Without appropriate direction, wanting very badly to achieve something may not be sufficient to get you there.

In the movie "Major League", Ricky Vaughn (played by Charlie Sheen), is determined to make it as a pitcher for the Cleveland Indians. He has a lot of natural talent, but still he hits everything but the plate! The coach knows that Ricky can't succeed like this, and eventually gets him to get his eyes checked. Sure enough, he needed glasses. After that, his fastball got the team the league championship, and through to the World Series!

I know that this is a rather literal example of "finding your direction", but even something as simplistic as this baseball story can illustrate several points:

- You need to know what outcome you want (for Ricky, it was to become a star pitcher)
- You need to know how to achieve this result (listen to the coach, support team strategies, and throw accurate pitches where the batter can't get a decent hit)
- You need to take the appropriate actions (consistently making pitches at 98mph. or more is somewhat helpful. So is being able to see the plate.)

So, as our example illustrates, with the right motivation, a good sense of direction, and the appropriate actions to make it happen, **success** results!

Now, how do we get that motivation?

Models of motivation

How do we motivate ourselves?

How do we get where we need to be?

Harnessing the Force

We could threaten ourselves with dire consequences...but that doesn't even work on other people. Why would it work on us? It's like setting your alarm clock 15 minutes ahead. You always know that the clock isn't telling you the truth so you ignore it. Not only do you sleep in the extra 15 minutes but you probably end up a half-hour late. You know the threats aren't real. So what happens? Nothing!

The problem with the stick is that it will eventually break or shatter — and we'll be left with no ability to motivate at all. We're much better off using the carrot. Keeping it positive, as it were. Focusing on delivering what is most valuable.

So how do you motivate yourself? The best answer to motivating yourself is "Exactly the same way you motivate anyone else."

Every manager understands the need to motivate the people who are working for him or her. The question is, "How do we do that?"

To get the details of how to motivate anyone, we use "models" of motivation. I want to emphasize something here. Models are simply neatly organized observations of how people react. These models are not theoretical constructs. They are a way to organize the results of hundreds or thousands of observations. We use these models to identify the different ways in which people can become motivated. We don't use them to explain why things happen the way they do — that's theory. Models are just an easy way to understand real life observations and their implications.

Using these models allows us to understand and (sometimes) to predict behaviors. Each model is an expression of actual results of observations — people really did behave this way in response to certain tests. Those results have been consolidated to give us guidance on the "what" and the "how", but they do not attempt to delve into the "why". That's not their purpose.

If you're a manager, you have a problem. You're trying to motivate an individual and you can't look inside their head. But with ourselves, we can look deep inside ourselves. We just try to avoid it. So the process of motivation is much simpler when applied to ourselves. We can ask ourselves if this or that will motivate us. We can acknowledge or refuse motivators. You don't need to be as rigorous or knowledgeable. You'll spot the mistakes and be able to correct them as you go. There's a big advantage to being able to read your target's mind.

For our purposes in self-motivation, we only need to look in detail at four models of motivation. The first one is Maslow's Hierarchy of Needs — This model helps establish priorities in the needs that motivate us. The second model is the Time Model.

This illustrates how time, and past experience, affects our motivation. Emotional Inertia is the third model. It explains why we don't always fight or take flight ... Emotional Inertia explains why we sometimes freeze in place. And finally, there is The Big Three Model (also known as "ASA"). It identifies the three most significant motivators for human activities.

Now let's look at each of these models and see what we can glean from them.

Maslow's "Hierarchy of Needs"

Let's start with the most important and complex of the models.

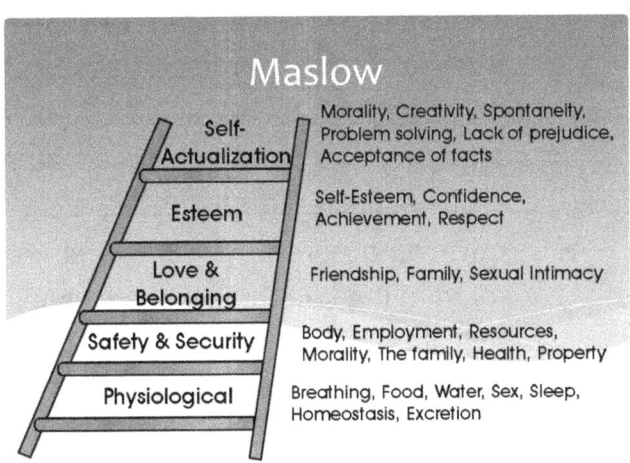

You've probably already heard about Maslow's Hierarchy. Abraham Maslow studied the needs and motivation of the top 1% of students, personalities, and thinkers during the 1930s and 40s. He introduced his "Hierarchy of Needs" in 1943, and completed and expanded it in his 1954 book *Motivation and Personality.*

Okay, fine. It's been around a long time. It's been the basis of motivational decisions for years. Who cares? What did Maslow say?

His basic concepts were:

- There are different levels of needs
- You can move through the different levels of needs
- You must first satisfy your needs at the lower level (e.g. for food, shelter, and safety) before moving up to higher level needs (e.g. the need to belong, the need for "self-actualization")
- Motivation occurs when an unmet need is offered at the current level and sometimes at a higher level
- As a need level is satisfied, it no longer motivates an individual (e.g. money often loses its motivating power when all the "comfort" needs are met. We

automatically think that money is the main motivator. But it really isn't. Once you reach a certain income level, it's just a way to keep score.)

Let's take an example to illustrate how Maslow's hierarchy works. In 2005, Hurricane Katrina decimated New Orleans, leaving 80% of the city flooded and thousands dead. There was almost 100 billion dollars in damages. It destroyed almost all of the state of Louisiana. After Katrina hit New Orleans, people were first seeking safety from the water. If you offered them food in their flooded homes, they would say, "Are you crazy! Get me out of here to somewhere safe." Once away from the water, the priority quickly became food and shelter. If all you could do was tell them, "You did a great job getting out of the boat, we really appreciate your cooperation", they would likely reply, "I've got to get some food right now."

And so on. As their lower level needs were met, they became motivated by the next level of needs.

That's part of what caused some of the problems — when the people in charge misjudged the motivations and offered something out of sequence. Or something that didn't matter yet. The people got a little testy. The response wasn't exactly positive — surprise, surprise.

Now that the people of New Orleans have moved back, their motivators have to do with recovering their lifestyle and the style of New Orleans. They've moved to the higher levels of need. Their needs for basic shelter, food, and survival met, those needs no longer motivate.

Maslow's "Hierarchy of Needs" is probably the best-known model for motivation. In Maslow's model, we strive to motivate people by meeting their higher-level needs. Those are needs at the levels of Love, Belonging, Esteem, and Self-actualization. In our context, lower-level needs are typically already being met, so they are not generally useful as motivators. In fact, if you check the top niches for internet marketing you'll find that niches directly related to those higher levels are the most profitable.

To use the hierarchy effectively there are some things you need to realize.

- To motivate, you must have an unsatisfied need at the current level, or at a higher level
- An unsatisfied need too far above your current level also won't motivate you (e.g. if you are worried about your personal safety, you are unlikely to be motivated by the possibility of one day writing a book)

- The key is to understand what level the individual is currently at
- Knowing the current level means that we can determine what will motivate an individual
- Variations have been proposed on the levels by various thinkers (e.g. Geert Hofstede has argued that the order in which the hierarchy is arranged is ethnocentric and the result of Maslow's focus on successful white Americans). Positioning "self-actualization" as the highest order need has also been suggested as the result of Maslow taking an "individualist" view

But since we're already ahead of the game — after all, we've got an unfair insight — we don't need to use any of the extensions to Maslow. Maslow's hierarchy is good enough for our purposes in directing us to identify specific motivators. In fact, we don't even have to get fancy with it.

Let's take a hypothetical example. I already know that my physical and security needs are being met. I have food, a job, a safe place to live and so on. However, maybe my relationship with my family is not what it should be. My belonging needs are not being met. So being able to spend more quality time with the family would motivate me. If my belonging needs are being met, then maybe the respect from being an author would be enough to motivate me. Do you notice that a number of self-help gurus seem to be focused on the "get your message out" sales pitch? Isn't that simply a case of focusing on the self-actualization level?

"Time and Motivation" model

The time and motivation model is a simple model about an important concept. It describes the implications that time has for motivation.

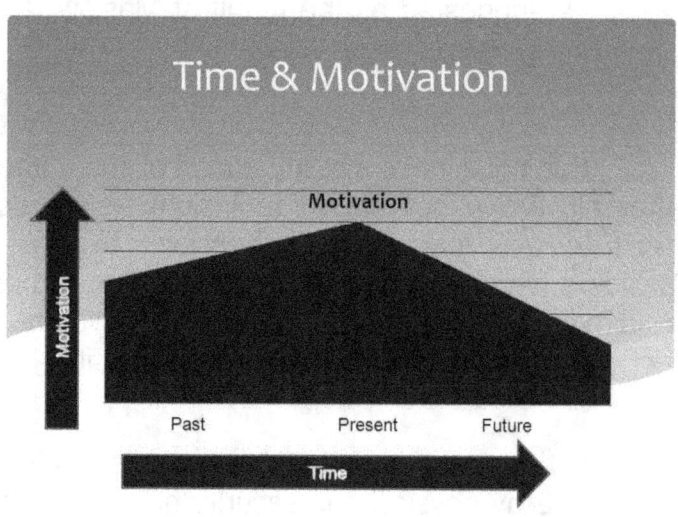

The model makes the following points:

- The closer you are to the present, the more motivation there is. The further away the less motivating it will be.
- Anything that has happened in the past will motivate you more than anything that might happen in the future — no matter how likely it is to occur.
- Anything that is happening now (i.e. a current situation) will motivate you the most
- The further back in the past something occurred, the less it will motivate you
- The further into the future something is expected to occur, the less it will motivate you

So if you want to motivate yourself the most, pick something that reflects what you're experiencing right now. If you can't do that then pick something that just happened. Failing that, then picking something that is just around the corner will work — maybe. Outside of that, the chances are it isn't going to be a strong enough motivator to work.

There is one weakness to this model. It doesn't really take into account any pre-existing and unresolved psychological damage, or its severity (e.g. untreated Post Traumatic Stress Disorder).

You see with conditions like PTSD, part of the problem is that the individual is continuing to react as if what has happened in the past is still occurring in the present. And therefore, the situation motivates as if it was a current problem.

But again, we're starting from a position of strength. Unless you have PTSD or something similar, for our purposes we can ignore these issues with the model. We can just use the concept as it stands. Of course, if you have PTSD or a similar issue, you should be dealing with a professional. Their insights will be critical both to your healing, and to determining what will provide motivation in your situation.

Let's take an example. Suppose that we had identified that both quality time with our children and spending time with our spouse were important. Last week, we had a fight with our children. Last month, we had a fight with our spouse. Next month, we expect to repeat our fight with our spouse. Which would be more important to us? Which would motivate us the more? Where would we focus our energies? Logically, we should be most worried about a fight with our spouse. After all, that's what will happen next. However, unless we were in the middle of a fight with our spouse, then spending time with our spouse would not be the most important and most motivating to us. In all the other cases, our relationship with our children would be the most motivating. The situation with our spouse would be less important to us or more correctly, would be less likely to be at the forefront of our minds.

"Emotional Inertia"

Have you heard about the Fight or Flight model? The basic concept of that model is that whenever we face a stressor, we react by fighting or fleeing. Our adrenalin levels go up, our breathing gets faster and our muscles prepare to save us. In short, we stress out. We prepare a physical reaction to an emotional threat and then end up with nowhere to direct the energy.

The problem with that model is that, in fact, most times we actually freeze. We neither fight nor flee. We just sit there and stare. The proverbial rabbit in the headlights.

But why?

That's where the emotional inertia model comes in.

Every task we tackle starts out hard. If we tackle it the right way, and remain motivated, it ends up easy. Cool. We can accept that intellectually.

But emotionally, accepting that truth is a different story.

Whatever our current emotional state is we are going to try to maintain it. The same thing applies with tasks. After all, they induce emotions. In order to get going on a task, we need some form of stimulus. We need something that will give us the energy to get over the initial resistance or hurdle. Otherwise, we will simply slide back into the state that we were in previously.

For example, if you are unhappy, you'd rather stay unhappy than change it to a happy state. I know that sounds silly but think about your own experiences. Have you ever been down in the dumps and just wanted to be left alone? Even though the people who were disturbing your "dumpitis" were trying to make you laugh, you probably yelled at them to leave. I know I have experienced that condition. In fact, I don't know anyone who hasn't. And the reverse is also true. If you're happy, you will try to avoid becoming sad. You may even find yourself laughing inappropriately. In order to initiate a change in your emotional state, you need to provide some form of push — such as motivation or emotional energy. That energy can be from an external source (someone else — your boss or spouse). However, it can also be provided by yourself. We call that self-motivation.

Resistance is always greater at the start or at a major stage change. You need a burst of energy to get over the hump.

Sitting down to write is harder than continuing to write.

Switching to edit mode is harder than continuing to write.

Now this is true whether we're talking about starting a task or moving through the emotional or decision continuums.

For our purposes, the Emotional Inertia model can be summarized in a single question. Do you have enough motivation to rise to the challenge, reach the summit, and start the easy descent to success confident in your abilities and your direction?

If not then you need to find that motivation ... and it needs to be more than just enough to keep you going. It needs to be enough motivation to get you off your duff and moving.

The "Big Three Motivators"

The final model we need to work with is the "Big Three" or ASA model.

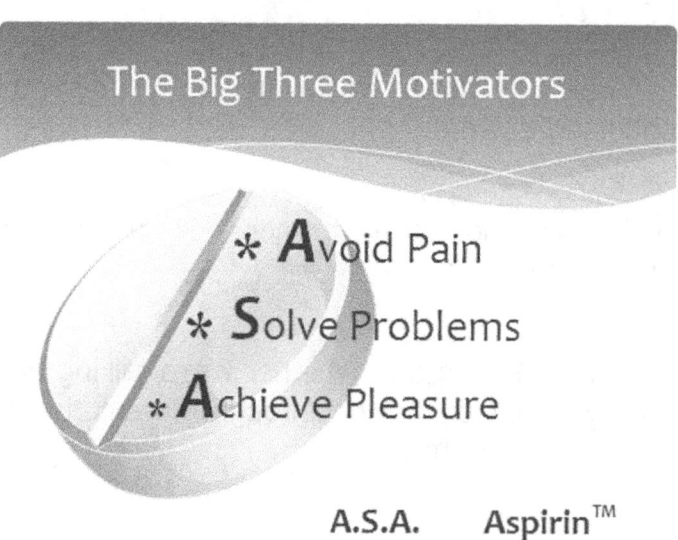

The Big Three Motivators

* **A**void Pain
* **S**olve Problems
* **A**chieve Pleasure

A.S.A.   Aspirin™

The "Big Three" model says to motivate someone there are three things that they *always* want:

- To **A**void pain
- To **S**olve problems
- To **A**chieve pleasure

The "Big Three" model is often used by marketers and in copywriting to attract new interest in a product or service offering. It's how copywriters motivate people. It's a simple and easy way to create interest. And it generally works.

I want you to buy my product. (Okay, yes, I really do. However, we're talking hypothetically here). To get you to buy my product, what I'm going to have to do is to motivate you to buy it. To make you want it, I need to identify an immediate problem you have. If I can then show you how my product will solve that problem, you'll want my product and you'll buy my product. If I can identify a current or future pain and then show you how my product will help you avoid it, the same thing happens. You'll buy my product.

Yes, I still have to overcome objections but I've crossed the threshold. In fact, if I can get you really wanting it, you'll even help me to convince you that the objections aren't important. You'll tell me what to say to convince you.

That's how the hard sell works. And also, why people hate it. The hard sell applies constant pressure to a motivator. As a result, the hard sell either hits the target and works right away — with the customer being carried along in the tsunami — or it misses the target and people react negatively to the constant push for a reaction. The soft sell does the same thing without pressure. If it hits the target, the customer reacts although it may take some time. If the sales spiel doesn't hit the target, the customer walks away without being turned off.

People are highly motived to avoid pain. If a particular course of action has even a *chance* of causing pain, then people will avoid it and look for pain-free alternatives. Even if those alternatives are actually less effective or efficient, or provide a less valuable result.

For example, politicians will often exaggerate the dangers of voting for any party other than their own. They'll describe in glowing terms the pain that choosing anyone other than them will bring. It's not a very nice tactic. And people often put it down. But there's a reason why politicians have always used it. Slamming your opponent is usually a very successful tactic, and can make people into very enthusiastic supporters of the "no pain" party!

Almost everyone gets a "kick" out of solving problems. It makes you feel competent, successful, and ready to take on more. It can improve your self-esteem and may attract attention and approval from others. All of which are motivators on their own. It gives you a warm glow of pleasure. And that warm glow is very motivating. But a problem is also a pain ... that's why it's a problem. So solving a problem is also motivating from the pain avoidance point of view. It's a win no matter how you look at it.

Finally, doing something that gives you a warm glow of pleasure is motivating. Just not as motivating as avoiding pain or solving problems. Anticipating pleasure in the future will motivate you to take action now (e.g. "I will write that article now, and bask in the positive feedback that it inspires"). Just not all that much motivation.

Some people are surprised to discover that problem solving is the most motivating technique. I just can't get myself to sit down and begin writing. How do I solve my problem? It was enough to motivate you, wasn't it? That's why you're reading this book. It was enough to motivate you to spend money, sit down, and read my book. And problems that are personal and current (like not having the time to write) are far more likely to get people actually moving towards finding a solution.

All that you need to do is link your solution (why you want to motivate) with an existing problem. I'm out of work and I need to find money. If I start writing, I'll earn enough to be okay. Linking those two thoughts may be all you need to motivate you to start writing. I want to spend time with the family. If I start writing, I'll be able to set my own hours. I can't stand the commute; writing will allow me to work from home. And so on, for whatever your chosen problem is.

Now unfortunately, this isn't a very positive model. In fact, it's pretty bleak. No one really wants to look on the dark side. The sad truth is that problems and pain are far more motivating than pleasure. The stick is stronger than the carrot. Making matters worse, is that ethically this model (or more correctly the situation it portrays) can be easily misused — and has been throughout history.

But even more unfortunately, the model is also true.

Typically, the "Big Three" model is used in conjunction with Maslow's "Hierarchy of Needs" model. The "Big Three" model tells you what to look for. Maslow's model tells you what to use when you find it, and gives you a number of hints where to look.

Figure it out first

So far, I have talked in generic terms, about how to motivate people in general. We have looked at generalized models of motivation. Now I need to get down to a more personal level. We need to talk about you.

This is necessary because motivation is *always* personal. What motivates you doesn't necessarily motivate me. What motivates me probably won't motivate you. That's why motivation is so difficult for a manager or a marketer. Everyone you talk to has a different set of motivators.

This difference may be because we each may be at a different level in the Maslow Hierarchy of Needs. It may also because we have had very different life experiences. We might well have been brought up in societies with very different histories (e.g. countries with decades of war and oppression and countries that have a history of peace), and with very different values (social, political, religious, etc.). One person might be motivated by an internal drive ("I've got to get my message out") while another might need external motivation (such as building a reputation).

Finding your own personal motivators requires you to sit down and figure out what *YOU* need. Use the models to help you identify what will motivate you. But remember that there is no "normal" here. There is only you, and what works for you.

Now be warned. This is not just listing the "it would be nice to have ..." items that come to your mind. You are looking for needs that, when satisfied, give you great pleasure, solve a current major problem, or enable you to avoid painful consequences. Just not in that order. You need to drive deep and be intensely honest with yourself. You may have to question every answer five times in order to drive down to the truth.

Satisfying those needs you identify, moves you towards self-actualization (the highest level in the Hierarchy of Needs). It will help you to become the best person you can be.

So the question becomes, "What *really* turns your crank?" Not just something you kind of want. Not just something that makes you feel some desire to write. Something that is really going to get you moving and writing. Even when the page is blank and threatening you.

Take me as an example. Initially I didn't describe myself as a writer. And I still seldom do. My resume talks about my project management skills, my problem solving abilities, my knowledge of complex technical environments, and so on. It doesn't say "dedicated writer" or "writeaholic" anywhere on it!

I had to discover that I am a natural-born writer all on my own.

So how did I make that discovery? I used the five steps that I'm going to talk about in a moment (or my own personal variant of them) to identify my need to write.

Life usually seems just way too busy. However, sometimes you just need to sit down, and take the time to get things clear. This clarity has to be achieved first, before you can successfully identify your true needs.

Finding your personal motivators starts off by:

- Getting into the habit of introspection.
- Clarifying in your own mind your dreams, desires, and aspirations
- Identifying your immediate problem ... your need.
- Identifying how writing a book will solve your immediate problem.
- Identifying the steps to your goal.

You will need to take some time for introspection. And you have to do it frequently. It's not something that will come naturally. Nor will it be particularly easy. You have to train yourself to dig into your heart and soul.

Stephen Covey said that you need to start with the end in mind. Your dreams, desires and aspirations are that end. You need to be clear on what they are. Your goals will need to guide you to make the right decisions in your life. Clarity will not come quickly or easily. You'll need to work on it.

Once you've identified your goal — your dreams, desires and aspirations — then you need to identify the problems that are stopping you from achieving those goals. Eliminating the biggest and most immediate problem will be the most motivating factor of all. That problem needs to be identified in order for it to become your major motivator.

But identifying the motivator isn't enough. You need to tie that motivator to the solution you have identified. So ask yourself, "Why is writing a book a solution?" and "In what way is writing a book a solution?" In short, you need to build a direct line from problem to solution to goal.

Finally, you need to identify the steps from problem to goal. You need to ask yourself, "What are the steps to get from where I am to where I want to be?" Why? So that you won't get lost and find yourself demotivated when the goal turns out to be further away than you had hoped. You need to manage your own expectations so that you don't become discouraged when those expectations hit the inevitable hiccup.

For example, in my case, I took a few weeks and sat down to think. I needed to decide if I wanted to continue to be a project management consultant. I needed to decide if I wanted to work for someone else. I needed to decide if I wanted to teach. Did I want to continue to create success out of failure? After all that's what a project management consultant does — and it is quite stressful. I needed to decide what was most important to me. What did I really care about? What path did I really want my life to take?

Once I knew where I wanted to go with my life, I needed to identify my biggest problem stopping me from getting there. That was a simple problem — I needed income. I needed to earn enough money to put food on the table. You see the job market had crashed and I didn't have any money coming in. Many of my clients had closed up shop and were looking for work themselves. I was up the proverbial creek and not only did I not have a paddle but the boat was leaking. I was about to lose my house. My family life was suffering from the stress. I was about to lose everything. So I needed to find income and I needed to find it quickly.

At this point, I had the first three steps. I had taken the time and I had decided what I wanted out of life. I had determined the problem that was stopping me — my motivator. Now I needed to figure out how to solve the problem. In my case, of course, I already knew the solution so instead I needed to figure out why writing is *the* solution to the problem. I needed to convince myself that writing is the solution and that other solutions just weren't as good.

Once I was sure that writing was the solution, I needed to set out a plan of attack. I needed a way to get from where I was — no income and bills piling up — to where I wanted to be — living off my writing and teaching.

The whole point here is to clarify what you want, what your motivating problems are, how writing will solve those motivating problems or avoid those motivating problems, and what you need to do to resolve those problems. The more clarity you can get in those areas, the more motivation you will have to actually sit down and write your book.

In short, sit down and figure out what your hot buttons are. That's what's going to push you to your goal.

Hot buttons and cold showers

When choosing your motivation, you need to remember one final element.

The greatest motivator is success.

However, the greatest demotivator is failure.

The purpose of motivation is to get you moving and keep you moving. It helps you to overcome blocks and difficulties. But when the relationship between the activity and achieving the motivator is broken, the motivation begins to fade. No matter how motivated you are when you begin, you will need to reinforce that motivation whenever you fail. In effect, your motivation is a bank account. Every time you motivate yourself, you add to that bank account. Every time you experience a difficulty or try to write, you draw from that bank account. You need to constantly top up your motivation bank account every time you use that motivation. The problem comes in when other factors can affect success or the relationship between writing and success is weak. You will end up drawing from the motivation account more often than you make deposits.

For example, you may be tempted to use money as your motivator.

However, writing a book does not automatically generate money. You still have to sell the book and, as we all know, writing a book does not guarantee you will sell it. Maybe your marketing isn't sufficient. Or people don't like your cover. Or your ability to write a proposal isn't good enough. Or maybe people just aren't buying that type of book right now. If your reason to write a book is based on money, you'll eventually stop writing books. Not because you aren't writing books successfully, but because the link between writing a book and making money is so tenuous.

Keep this in mind when choosing your motivator. If other factors can affect your success in solving your problem, then solving that problem has a limited motivational life. You may have to choose multiple motivators.

Four tricks

When you have gone through the intense process of determining your unmet needs, the ones you absolutely, totally want to achieve as a priority, then those are your ultimate motivators.

Now you need to figure out how to activate those motivators. You are seeking motivation to achieve your identified needs, in a reasonable timeframe, and to the greatest extent possible. You need to figure out how to drive that motivation home.

If you're motivated externally, it's easy. Just tell someone. Become accountable to someone else. You can do this by telling others what you're going to produce and when, what you have done, or by setting a deadline. For example, you might schedule an exchange editing session, or you might arrange to drop off your writing. Basically, you're suckering someone into becoming your boss. Writers groups are great for this type of motivation.

Unfortunately, external motivation can usually only take you so far. After a certain point, people become defensive and angry when they are externally motivated and unable to achieve. They feel guilty and are so uncomfortable that they express that discomfort in negative emotions. That's why the driving boss is so hated. Most people hate being bad and they take it out on the person who is perceived to be sitting in judgment.

The solution for the problems with external motivation for most people is to build up internal motivation. You are doing this for yourself. You have only yourself to blame. And only yourself to report to. Of course, you do have to apply a little internal discipline with the motivation. But that's a minor price to pay.

When I am leading a team the first speech I give them is how to work with me. I tell them that the key to working with me is twofold. The first and most important is to set a behavior standard for themselves that is higher than I expect from them. That way, they will be motivated to be better than I expect. I won't have to discipline them. All I have to do is help them achieve. And we'll both be happy. This is what you are going to try to do to yourself.

The process of achieving the results you desire is likely to be a fairly long process. As you diligently follow this process, you will want to continually reinforce to yourself just what that set of goals entails. You want to keep that vision of total achievement always at the front of your mind. After all, you won't have me to hound you.

That's the definition of advertising isn't it? Keeping your message at the front of your target's mind. In this case, the message just happens to be your message, the advertising is your advertising, and the target's mind is your mind. You're both the target and the source.

There are many alternative ways of advertising where you are going and what you will achieve, but here are three good ones that work for most people:

- Signs

- Rewards
- Active Visualization

Trick #1: You can't forget

Advertisers have used signs to motivate buyers for centuries. From the placard to the ubiquitous billboard, signs of all types are used because they work. And they can work just as effectively when the message is personal motivation. Signs can help to remind you of why you need to write, even when you have many reasons not to write. They can feed on your guilt. They can boost your mood when writing is the last thing you want to do. They can soothe hurt feelings when life gets too hard on you.

Start by listing out why you need to write your book. Then for each reason create a short one-phrase reminder of that reason. Better still use one word. Try not to use a full sentence, as this will be too long. You are unlikely to read it. For example if one of your motivators is being able to spend more quality time with your family, all you need to remind yourself is the word "family" and "time".

Now look for pictures illustrating the concepts for you. For example, pictures of a clock will illustrate time. Pictures of your family will help to illustrate the concept of family. Try to choose pictures that illustrate the situation you are using to motivate yourself. For example, a picture of the family at Disneyland or on a picnic can illustrate quality family time.

Now create a series of signs for those concepts. You might create a large collage, for example. Or a miniature billboard illustrating the major motivator for writing. Or simply use a set of post it notes with one word in large letters. In fact, you'll need several different types of signs. Most likely, you'll need a different size for each application.

Now post the signs everywhere you look during the day. The key here is to bombard yourself constantly with visual reminders of why you need to write. Place a large sign near your work area. Post-it notes work great almost everywhere else including computer screens and bedroom doors. Post-it notes also have an advantage in that they are small and less offensive than a full-sized sign. Your spouse is therefore less likely to get mad at you for putting Post-it notes all over the house including on the refrigerator or on the washroom mirror. On the other hand, sticky notes (which is the generic term for the ubiquitous 3M Post-it notes) aren't as easy to see. This makes them easier to ignore so you may find quantity is as much a spousal irritant as size.

One variation on the sign is the so-called "Vision Board". These signs have been the topic of a great deal of conversation on television and in other media lately. A vision board is a specific type of sign that combines visual clues to all the goals you are hoping to achieve. All the reasons you are writing in one collage. For example, you might have a picture of the home you want to buy or the sailboat. Maybe you'll have a picture of your family on that vacation you've always wanted. These are your goals. Whatever you expect writing to bring you belongs on your vision board.

Trick #2: Self-inflicted pats

One of the first things that we learn is the joy of getting a reward. We learn as children to anticipate Christmas or our birthdays (or whatever your culture's gift giving season is) because of the gifts we receive. Later we learn to enjoy them for the gifts we can give (and the joy those gifts bring). The concept of effort and reward is central to our thought process as managers. It's one of those tools that is so much a part of the core that it is often overused and misused. However, it has a very powerful effect when used as a self-motivation tool. In effect, for self-motivation, it is both an internal and an external motivator.

Using a reward as a self-motivator is a three-step process.

You begin by choosing the effort you wish to reward and the reward you will offer. The reward must be worth the amount of effort involved. However, keep in mind that the true reward is the recognition that accompanies that reward. This is as true for you when self-motivating as it is when used by a manager. Making a big issue about rewards for achievement is a key element in the value of a reward as a motivator.

Rewards do not have to be large. When I finish a book, I may take my wife out for a special dinner. Or I might be a big spender and buy a Kindle book that I really want to read. I remember in the distant past, a manager who used a silly $2.99 statue as a reward. Whoever won the month's goal got to keep the statue on their desk. What matters is that you are rewarding the behavior. The size of the reward is almost irrelevant.

However, the reward does have to matter to you. It has to be worth the effort involved in your eyes. Only in your eyes. No one else's opinion matters. So choosing a reward that you don't value won't work. For example, if you are always eating out, taking your spouse out for dinner won't work as a reward. Why? You do it all the time anyway so that particular reward isn't going to be valued.

Rewards do not have to be all or nothing affairs. In fact, when choosing your reward you are much better to select a number of tiny rewards to be awarded at each stage in the process, than to select one big reward at the end. Celebrating each stage will always achieve better progress than holding off to the end. The shorter the stage the more effective the motivation. For example, let's say that you have set a reward of buying that big screen television when you finish your book. Now compare that to a reward of being able to watch an hour of television when you finish the day's work. Which will be more motivating? The hour of television. It sounds silly but that's the way our minds work. Constant repetition wins out over quality.

The second task is to ensure you are constantly aware of the effort and reward. Use a sign to reinforce the reward. Paste a sticky note with the effort and reward on your work surface or computer screen. In fact, the most successful method of advertising is to combine this advertisement with the next task.

The third task is to measure your progress. This has the effect of keeping you on track and motivated. And it acts as a reinforcement of the effort/reward relationship — effectively ensuring that you are both made aware and motivated with a single act.

More than that, it raises the bonus of competition. For example, let's say that you are tracking the number of words written in a day. You reward for four thousand words per day ready for the editor. If you track the number of words, you may find four thousand in the first day and four thousand one hundred on the next. The day after, it may increase to four thousand four hundred. Even if it falls to below four thousand the day after that, you are far more likely to exceed four thousand five hundred on day five than if you had not tracked the number of words. Getting through more words than the day before becomes a game — a game you want to win.

One technique that works wonders is to create a chart showing the days and the goal measurement with a picture of the reward placed at the appropriate points on the chart. So for example, you might have a chart showing days and number of chapters. Place a picture of a book you want on the third chapter point for each day to indicate a reward after two chapters. As you finish chapters, mark it off on the chart. You'll soon find yourself finishing off three, four, or more chapters in a day. Of course, there is a limit but you will constantly stretch that limit as you begin to compete with yourself.

If you choose to reward yourself after a number of steps (let's say after the final chapter is written) then you need to track progress up to that point. In that case, a progressive chart showing achievements by day as well as the current progress works best. However, this does require you to track multiple achievements. For example, you might track the number of chapters written per day. At the same time, you might track total number of chapters written to this point. The picture of your reward would be placed at the point where you expected the reward to be earned on the total line — in this case, day 5, chapter 10. The key is to make the relationship between effort and reward, and the progress toward the reward, as clear and obvious as possible.

Trick #3: Creating a crystal ball

Earlier in this section, we talked about Vision Boards as a means to advertise your motivation to yourself. But there is more involved in Vision Boards than just reinforcement of motivation reasons.

For many years, gurus have been promoting the technique called Visioning or Visualization under many names. Whether you call it visioning, visualization, self-programming or neuro-linguistic programming (NLP), this is a technique that frankly sounds like magic. And in fact, many of the writers on the subject have ascribed magical capabilities to the process. This is especially true of early 20th century self-help writers who believed in the scientific validity of magic. But it really isn't magic. It isn't daydreaming. And it really does work.

The proper term for what I am recommending is Active Visualization. The basic process is simply a matter of programming yourself and then activating that programming. You do so with four steps:

1. First you predict the future
2. You see the outcome
3. You practice achieving that outcome in your mind (visualize it)
4. Then you do it — successfully the first time

Now I want to be clear, this is not daydreaming about being successful. This isn't simply visualization of the end result and having that result magically appear once you really believe it. That doesn't work. I'm talking about getting your target and the way you are going to get to that target absolutely clear in your mind. And that includes identifying and overcoming obstacles. Then practicing until you have your actions down pat. This is a way of planning, clarifying your plans, and focusing your actions. In many ways, it is a simplified version of project management.

My son and daughter used to take Karate, so I like to use an example from Karate. If you've ever seen a black belt demonstrate on television, or seen a Kung Fu movie you've seen this technique illustrated. I'm talking, of course, of breaking a 1" thick solid pine board with the heel of your hand —

on your first try. While children are not allowed to use real boards, the truth is anyone can do it safely — even if you don't know a gi from an obi or from a dojo. Here's how.

Have someone hold the board out from their body, at a little below shoulder height (you don't want to hit them!) Prepare to twist your body and extend your arm so that the heel of your hand will strike the center of the board. Close your eyes and visualize the board breaking and your hand moving through the broken board to a point a foot or so beyond the location of the board.

This last part is critical. And it's why children aren't allowed to use real boards. If you visualize your hand stopping at the board, then it will stop there. And the board will not break. Your hand on the other hand …

When you visualize your hand travelling through the board as it breaks, then you achieve the exact outcome that you saw. The board splits into two or more pieces, splinters may fly, the person holding the board may even be unable to hang on to it. Your mind has already created the result, and now your body just follows orders!

Then practice the result slowly. Slowly perform the movement of your hand striking the board without actually impacting the board. Simply connect with the board and stop. Continue visualizing it moving through the board and out the other side. Feel your arm stopping four to six inches beyond the board. Going slowly helps you do this. Repeat the movements until you can see the movement clearly in your mind.

This is an example of how Active Visualization creates what we call muscle memory. Of course, muscles don't really have memory cells. What we are really doing is implanting a habit and a process in our memory. The mind then activates that memory of how to achieve the result when it is called upon to do so.

You can do this same process with almost anything. Athletes do this as part of their normal training. Professional golfers do it. Olympic swimmers do it. NHL hockey players do it. And you can do it with your writing, your business, and your life.

From a motivation standpoint however, you only need to see that end goal clearly. That end goal that you have visualized achieving. The benefits of that end goal will help you gain the energy you will need to expend the effort to achieve them. Knowing the steps in between — memorizing the process to gain your goals — is a bonus.

Your assignment if you choose to accept it

This chapter was all about increasing your desire to write. Your motivation or desire will carry you through and help you to achieve when everything else is fighting against you. At this point, I hope you are building an appreciation of just how much you can achieve when you are just where you need to be and you are motivated for success.

However, motivation isn't the only part of the problem with finding time to write. In the next chapter, I will cover information that you can use to reduce your writing effort dramatically. And reduced effort means more writing is achieved in the time available. And it also means that your motivation isn't burned away overcoming the writing process.

In most cases, using a well-defined writing system will also give you better quality and more consistency in your writing projects.

In the meantime, you may want to stop reading for a short period. Go through the steps to identify your motivators — your hot buttons. Decide how you are going to reinforce your motivation. Visualize the results and the process of getting there.

When your motivation has been boosted way beyond what you thought possible, you'll be ready to find out how to reduce your need for motivation.

"This is how you do it: you sit down at the keyboard and you put one word after another until it's done. It's that easy, and that hard."
— **Neil Gaiman**

Chapter 4:

Making Writing Easier

The power of systems

In the last chapter, I looked at the issues involved in motivating yourself (or others) to write. I discussed four models of motivation. More importantly, I discussed how you can use them to identify the needs in you that will most strongly motivate you (called your "motivators"). I also suggested some ways to activate those motivators. Hopefully, the "three tricks" proved to be useful in boosting your own motivation.

Remember the Work Equation? The three keys to actually sitting down to write are desire, effort (or more correctly reduced effort) and available time. Now that we've built up the desire to write, it's time to take on the other side of the potential for writing portion of the equation. The other side of the coin from motivation is to reduce the effort involved in writing — making it easier to write.

Think of it like a car. You put gasoline in the car and you drive it to your destination. Along the way, depending on the distance and your vehicle, you may have to fill your gasoline tank again.

In our illustration, the gasoline is your desire to write. By building up your desire, you have put more gasoline in your own tank. How much will you need? Well, just as a poorly maintained clunker will need more gasoline to get there than it would if it was a well-maintained, modern hybrid vehicle, so you need more desire if your writing system is less efficient (or effective).

You see, between the desire to write and the effort to write is where procrastination occurs. Available time is only a limitation. To overcome procrastination, we need to both increase our desire to write and make it easier to write. By achieving both those results, we are less likely to find things that prevent us from accomplishing our work. In other words, starting and finishing our writing. We're far less likely to procrastinate.

In the next three chapters, I will focus on information that you can use to dramatically reduce your writing effort. This reduction has a great impact on your writing achievements. When the task of writing becomes easier, the "drag" on your motivation as a result of the writing effort is reduced. This leads directly to writing more in the same amount of time (and sharply reduces "writing weariness"). Along the way, it's going to help you avoid writer's block. I will do this by focusing on your writing system.

Now don't get overwhelmed by the term "writing system". All I am talking about is how you write — the process itself. However, a system goes beyond a mere step-by-step process. A system takes into account your environment, your work habits and anything else that can affect how you write. It's the holistic version of step-by-step directions. In this chapter, we're going to focus on the process. In the next two chapters, we'll deal with the other factors.

Now here's the kicker ... you're going to have a writing system whether you want one or not. Writing isn't a single task. It's a series of tasks. And no matter how much you try, you are going to need to be somewhere when you write. And that somewhere is going to affect your writing. You are doing the work. How you work will affect your writing. In order to write a book, you are going to have to develop a system to do it. Now you can create a new system for every book you write. Or you can have one system that you constantly improve.

Having a well-defined writing system has several advantages. It means you can get better. It means you can build in quality. It can make the work easier. We're going to explore those advantages in more detail in just a moment.

On the other hand, it does have two disadvantages. The first is that it requires discipline. Saying that you have a writing system isn't enough. You have to apply it without unintended modification.

The second disadvantage is that it requires you to put aside your undisciplined approach. Yes, horror of horrors, you need to change. You need to recognize that doing things by the "seat of the pants" method is neither efficient nor effective.

Let's face some facts here, the business of writing — from identifying the need for a writing "product" to delivering the final product, is long and complex. And it is more than just a simple sequential process with a set of checkpoints. Like any business, your ability to perform repeatedly is one key to your success. And the system (or process) you use is the key to delivering your product repeatedly.

In this chapter, I'm going to explore some of this complexity and show you what to look for in a writing system (and what to avoid). I will end this chapter with an example, so you can see how some of those characteristics will appear in a finished system.

Now, it's time for a confession. I have a writing system that I have developed and sell called the "Content Mapping System". You can find it at http://www.LearningCreators.com and in book form at http://www.LearningCreators.com/products/buyebook.
It works extremely well when you are writing how-to-books and other non-fiction books and eBooks. It doesn't work for fiction.

I'm going to use our system for the example. HOWEVER, there are a number of other systems available. Including a customized, informal system you might patch together yourself. This isn't meant to be a sales brochure. The reason I am mentioning our system is to show you some examples of how the underlying writing needs can be implemented. That way you can know what a good system looks like. It's simply that I know what to look for, so I made sure those characteristics appear in our system. Therefore, it just makes sense to use our system to demonstrate the right characteristics. Besides, it's easier.

The content map won't work for fiction. However, the needed characteristics for both fiction and non-fiction writing systems are the same. So if you write fiction, you can still use this list to find your own best system. It just won't be mine.

Why is your system = your success?

So why do you need a writing system?

I've mentioned some of the reasons already. But the truth is they are more or less minor advantages when compared to the one big advantage of having a formal writing system.

Now let me explain something here. All I mean by a formal system is one that is well defined and well understood. It should be written down, preferably as a flow diagram of some type. However, it doesn't have to be. All it really needs to be formal, is that you know exactly what you are doing, when and why. Writing it down is simply a way to achieve that goal.

So what's the big advantage of a formal writing system? Ready for this? You can change it over time. Hopefully. to achieve better and better results, but always with control over the change.

It sounds silly, but with an informal or poorly defined system, the way you do things morphs over time. You don't change it. It changes all on its own.

Making Writing Easier

In fact, it is very difficult to intentionally change it. None of us drops old habits or develops new habits easily. We're all somewhat lazy. All of us, no matter how disciplined we think we are. So we tend to forget to complete tasks. Not only that, but there is a process sometimes called "the expert effect" or "comfort effect", which compounds this tendency.

When we start the learning process, we aren't aware that we don't know something or that we are doing things incorrectly. Something happens to cause us to become aware of our ignorance and the learning cycle begins. We learn more and eventually become very aware of the information. After a period of time, we internalize the topic and no longer need to be aware of the information. We become experts. We no longer have to refer to references or memory aids. We can do it in our sleep. Unfortunately, that drop in awareness causes us to ignore what and how we do the process. It's automatic. We aren't as careful as we used to be. We forget. Mistakes begin to creep in and become part of the process. Eventually the mistakes become an issue and the cycle begins once again. In learning theory, this is sometimes called the learning cycle. (Then again, just about everything is referred to as the learning cycle!)

This is why an informal system is less effective than a formal system over time. With a well-defined system you decide what, where, and when to make a change. It is a decision, not just a mistake, or a case of "it's easier that way". And as we all know, the easy way seldom really is.

In fact, a formal system will slowly improve over time. You may occasionally make a mistake in judgment or try something that doesn't work. You will occasionally forget and do things wrong. But over time, your good judgment will win out. Changes that work will be incorporated into your system. The bad parts will be intentionally replaced. The system will slowly begin to better match your way of doing things.

But that's not all.

Experience has also shown that using a well-defined writing system is also likely to give you better quality and more consistency in the end result whatever variety of writing projects you undertake. It helps you to achieve a better initial result. It also allows you to identify (or it provides) specific checks and balances. Between the two — better initial product and better editing — the result is a better book or eBook produced faster and with less time wasted in rewrites and other wasted efforts.

Writing systems achieve a tremendous number of benefits for writers, and can actually create success.

Why can they create success?

Consider the situation of building a car. Let's say, you built a car from scratch by propping up some wheels in the dirt and then trying to add panels, doors, a windshield, an engine, etc. The result would be a pile of bits, and great frustration for the would-be car builder. Cars are not built that way for a reason (and that applies to washing machines and toasters too). Everything in the modern world is designed to meet the needs for which it was intended and to be easy for the builder. And profitable. If not it tends to fail in the marketplace.

In fact, one of the causes of the destruction of the British car industry was that they had a hard time switching from a bits and pieces car manufacturing process to a systematic process. They kept trying to build the whole thing at once rather than in series of well-defined steps. They couldn't learn the lesson that Henry Ford is famous for. They couldn't make the leap from individual artisans doing the whole job to a process. They relied on the individual to overcome the system and produce quality rather than relying on the system to produce quality. And people, as we all know, have good days and bad days. As a result, between quality and cost — British cars simply couldn't compete.

Car building starts with determining needs. Then comes designing for those needs. Next is building the basic structure and then completing the fleshing out of that framework — with body panels and trim, seats and cup holders, lights and controls. At each stage, the assembly is checked for quality. Finally, the whole vehicle is checked to ensure that everything is assembled properly, and is working correctly. The result is a quality car, built as inexpensively as it can be.

A writing project is not a car. No one would claim that it is. However, a car is built more efficiently and effectively using a systems approach, than a haphazard one. Similarly, a book or even an article can also be built using a systems approach. This brings major benefits to the builder — or writer in this case. Some folks feel that it also gives a better product to the consumer — your reader. And I admit — after having read as many free eBooks as I have — that I'm firmly of the same opinion. There is a definite correlation between a good writing system and a well-written book. Before you can create great art, if you even want to create great art rather than simply a good book, you must be good at your craft. And the writing system you use is part of your craft.

As I indicated before, you're going to have a writing system regardless of your wishes. The business of writing is just too complex to live without one.

One alternative is to invent a new process for every book or piece you have. Every book will have its own process. You are constantly in a cycle of process creation by experimentation. Never learning from your previous efforts. Not only do you have to be prepared to fail with an experimental change but also you need to be prepared to fail on every book you write. After all, every new book is an experiment in process design.

Another alternative is to start without a system. In this case, you will need to invent a process on the fly, just as you did in the first alternative. However, rather than doing a new version for every book, you will keep that system for the next book. Then you will continually modify the system when it doesn't deliver what you had hoped for. There is nothing wrong with developing your own system, but it will take time, experience, and experimentation. And experimentation means a high risk of failure. You have to be prepared to fail if you are going to experiment. That's true whether you are talking about a writing system, or an accounting system, or a marketing system.

The third alternative is to pick an existing writing system. You can pick one that meets your needs, or you can stumble into it. But, even if you buy a system, you're going to adjust it to meet your own needs and style. This customization is natural and it is healthy. In fact, you should be building that change into your own system regardless of its source.

Your writing system can make writing a book either hard or easy. It needs to be matched to your writing. In fact, you may even need more than one system if you do more than one type of writing.

Some systems are designed specifically for learning content. Some systems are designed for writing book length fiction. However, most writing systems are designed for journalism ... or writing short pieces. Which is great if you want to write a newspaper article or magazine piece. Not so great if you are writing a self-help book or a product manual or a novel.

Why? Because, most new writers want to write the Great <your nation here> Novel. They want to write fiction. So the creators (or marketers) of writing systems focus on selling the systems that most people want or need.

On the other hand, many professional writers are focused on the short piece. Specifically on journalism or magazine style writing. Both of these markets kept many writers employed, solvent and happy for many years. Certainly, more than either fiction or non-fiction books did. Many of those individuals are now hawking their particular techniques for keeping their bosses happy and cranking out the words. After all, there aren't that many places hiring out-of-work journalists currently.

Unfortunately, having a great system for the wrong type of writing is still going to give you a poor system. Each of these types of writing - books versus short pieces, fiction versus journalism versus time-based non-fiction versus learning content — have different base characteristics. And require extremely different tools and techniques.

For example, a book is far more complex than a short piece.

A book needs a map in order to complete it in a reasonable period. You need to know where you are going and when. After all, you're going to be writing for at least 40 hours or more. You need to be able to remember where you are and what you had intended to say.

A short piece — such as a newspaper article or an essay — is finished very quickly. Typically in less than an hour. In fact, some systems look to produce the typical article length of 250 to 500 words within fifteen minutes to half an hour. Having a step-by-step map of the article is often a case of overkill. At most, you need a list of the points you want to make. The overheads of developing a complex paragraph-by-paragraph outline would overwhelm an article. That's why you were taught to outline in school. All you were writing were short pieces. And such a rudimentary writing system as outlining was still sufficient to produce the longest of those pieces.

Similarly, fiction brings together character, location or scene, and actions to create a story. It is a complex, multi-dimensional amalgamation. On the other hand, learning content is simply a matter of organizing facts and presenting them in a way that is easily understood and meets your readers' needs.

By the way, learning content is a fancy term for course material. I'm not going to get into the philosophical reasons for the term here. There are valid reasons to refer to it as learning content rather than training materials or one of the other common terms. We're really talking about the same thing. It also doesn't matter what the media is. Books, eBooks, videos, audios, webinars, podcasts, and seminars all carry this type of content. If it helps any — use the word self-help book whenever I say learning content.

Unfortunately, each of these types of writing has different requirements. The tools and techniques that work best are different for each of them. Storyboarding works great for fiction writing, however, it doesn't work for learning content. Similarly, Content Maps work great for learning content but don't really help for fiction.

When selecting your system — or building your own — you need to know what types of writing you will be doing. You will need a different system for each type of writing. If you choose the wrong system for your writing, then you will find yourself expending a great deal of effort and not achieving the goal.

The wrong system means that you are relying entirely on your skill as a writer to succeed. You cannot help but fail occasionally. After all, you'll be playing the risk game without any weapons to help you. Failure is an ever-present risk at the best of times. But without a system helping you, it will occur more frequently. And worse, it means that you will always be working harder than necessary even when you do succeed.

A good, well-matched system on the other hand, will help you to succeed. It will build in the steps, checks and balances you need to ensure success. It will build in the steps, checks, and balances to ensure that you produce a quality book.

Remember that a professional writer can't afford to fail. As a professional writer, your time is money. You can't afford to spend a week or a month or six months writing a book that you can't or won't finish. Failure is not an option. That's why so many professionals follow a formal writing system.

Your writing system is an expression of your discipline and craft. It turns your creativity into a finished product. There is no luck or art involved in the production. Only in the initial creation. It makes sure that you have what you need when you need it and that you produce the result you desire. It adds the discipline and craft to your writing so that you can deliver art to your readers and not just envision it.

What to look for

I write learning content. I do not normally write fiction. I did write fiction long ago, so I am familiar with how it differs from learning content. I do not write journalistic pieces. I do frequently write short learning content articles. However, most of my writing is for the purposes of delivering book-length learning content.

I will, however, try to keep the following discussion at a fairly high level so that it applies to everyone who is writing a book. And that includes real eBooks. Generally speaking, it will be overkill for short pieces.

So, as I walk through the following points, please keep that in mind. If you write a different type of book (such as novels) then your system may have some different needs.

Making Writing Easier

When you are writing to teach somebody something, you need to have a writing system that is designed to produce learning content (not memoirs, sci-fi, or kids' books). Having the system matched to the type of book you produce is probably the most important requirement. Which is why I spent so much time talking about it in the previous section. That's also why I will keep repeating it.

What makes a system for learning content books good?

There are seven characteristics of a good learning content writing system:

1. Process decomposition
2. Detailed description of elements
3. Recognition of different variations of tasks
4. Isolation of different types of thinking
5. Use of cognitive tools
6. Appropriate level of detail
7. Builds in consistent quality

Firstly, it needs to break the process into small tasks. The smaller, the better. Breaking the process up into small parts helps to ensure that you perform each of the tasks. After all, if you keep skipping tasks, your system will soon fail to produce a quality book.

Writer's Block Demolition

Secondly, each of those tasks needs to be properly explained and separated. It can't hide a part of the work in a bundle. For example, on its own, the instruction to "create an outline" doesn't help much. You need a system that tells you how to create an outline. And the steps involved.

The third point (variations on tasks) is related to this detailed description. There is a need to separate the tasks involved. This is especially true with editing. There are many different types of editing. If your system combines them or fails to distinguish between them, then you'll find yourself being very inefficient. For example, traditionally the structural edits (that is have I got the points in the right order) are done after the writing as part of the final edit. A change in structure at that point forces you to completely rewrite the book.

The need to separate thinking types continues this theme. Tasks need to be isolated by the type of thinking involved in the task. There is a fallacy that seems to be prevalent now. In fact, it's used to justify working frantically. I'm talking about the concept of multitasking. Trying to multitask and efficiency are not related. In fact, the brain doesn't multitask at all. It just switches quickly. So quickly, we often don't realize that we've had to stop one mental task and start again. Quickly of course being a relative term. The brain doesn't actually switch quickly. You just don't consciously notice the time required. Your brain needs to come to a full stop and then shift gears. Compared to the speed at which it normally functions, this stop and start mental processing is extremely slow. As a result, the more switching, the less efficiently the overall task is performed. And the more tired it leaves you.

For example, retrieval of information, organizing information, and editing of information are three different tasks as far as your brain is concerned. Do one and the brain is in its glory. Try to do several of them at once, and the process seems to take forever. Why? Because your brain needs to stop and then start up again as it changes from one task to another. It doesn't like doing it. It isn't efficient and it leaves you feeling tired and overworked.

Point number five (cognitive tools) is also related to how the brain works. In this case, however, you aren't avoiding doing things the brain isn't good at doing. Instead, you are using methods that work with the brain's functions. These tools are called Cognitive Tools. And your system should center around the use of one or more of these tools.

There are many possible cognitive tools that can be used. Given the nature of writing, there is one class of tool that is most often used. These are generically called Semantic Network Diagrams. That's a big long title. However, an SND is simply a network diagram that links ideas, concepts, and words. The most well-known version is the line-centric SND. You most likely have heard of it as mind mapping. This technique was promoted by a British psychologist by the name of Tony Buzan in the mid-1970s. But there are other versions including the node-centric SND and numerous hybrid variations. Once you know how to work with one SND, then all you need is to learn the differences. The process is similar although the details will vary.

And of course, there are still other tools which perform the same functions.

There is one commonly used writing tool that doesn't qualify as a cognitive tool. Making a list isn't a cognitive tool. In fact, it fights the mind. Remember that a cognitive tool works with the mind. Cognitive tools are almost always diagram based. At the very least, they work with the mind's ability to see a pattern. Pictures help you to see patterns. Outlines don't help you to see patterns.

For example, a cognitive tool doesn't ask you to organize while you are retrieving information. Instead, a cognitive tool may help by providing the organization for you. A cognitive tool also doesn't try to edit the information while you are retrieving the information. However, a cognitive tool may provide a self-editing form where the nature of the tool provides some types of editing.

Making Writing Easier

A list or outline, unfortunately, does none of that. It forces your brain to do all the work at once. It asks you to retrieve, sort, and edit all at the same time. Otherwise, you end up with a list that's too long and too difficult to work with. As a result, your brain is constantly switching between tasks. Lists can be incorporated into cognitive tools as a recording device. For example, brainstorming produces a list of ideas for later review. However, on their own lists are not cognitive tools.

The next point is that the system must produce the appropriate level of detail. In the case of a system for short pieces, that could be as simple as a list of the points to make. However, in the case of a book, you really need a system that will create an outline at the paragraph level. You can produce 100 words on a single point reasonably easily (in other words an average paragraph). However, if you produce less detail you will find yourself forgetting what needs to be written during the writing portion. As a result, you will be forced to retrieve, organize, and edit information at the same time you are producing the words. The result will be extra work and an increase in the effort required.

Finally, the system you choose must produce a consistent quality of book. If you've been involved in business at all over the last 20 years then you've heard the term quality management. ISO 9000 was big in the 1990s. Six Sigma and Lean are two big ones right now. So is ITIL. A whole big mess of similar acronyms are being used by managers the world over, all of which are simply variations on the same theme.

But what do we mean by producing consistent quality? What is that in practical terms?

Modern quality management systems include two different types of quality related tasks.

Quality control tasks are what we typically recognize as testing. They occur after the work has been completed. Quality control tasks are used to verify that the product meets the required quality. In writing, editing has traditionally been a quality control task. Although to be honest, in the real world, editing tends to have more characteristics of rework than of quality control.

Quality assurance tasks are focused on improving the quality of the product during the production of that product. Typically, they occur either before or during the production process.

Writing systems have traditionally focused on quality control. That's why rewrites are so much a part of the tradition of writing. However, as we've learned in other processes, your writing system needs to include quality assurance elements. These elements ensure that quality is built into your book. Even more importantly, they help to improve the efficiency and ease of use of your writing system by reducing rework. (In writing rework is usually referred to as writing multiple drafts). And they help to ensure that your book is of value to the reader — meaning they are likely to buy it. Quality assurance helps to ensure that the right quality control elements are placed at the right points within the process to ensure that the best quality results.

Now to repeat — at the risk of sounding like a broken record ...

None of this matters if your system doesn't have the right focus at all.

Your system must be focused on producing the types of books that you produce (learning content in my case) NOT generic writing. Fiction is different from non-fiction. Time-based or event-based information (fiction, history) is different from fact-based.

Any Time-based piece is a story ... so at some point, it needs to use some form of a storyboard.

Fact-based writing is simpler — it is just data retrieval & organization, so it needs a tool that focuses on retrieval, editing and organizing the information.

These are only the most important elements by the way ...

Example of a writing system

Okay so let's take an example and show you how those characteristics are included.

I want to be clear that this is an example using the Content Mapping system. This is not a sales brochure. Even if it occasionally sounds like it is. What follows is just an example for your guidance. There are many other writing systems, some of which are just as good. The Content Mapping system is focused on creating learning content. In fact, we use a learning content methodology as the base of our system. The process comes out of developing teaching materials (i.e. learning content) in any media, not from the profession of writing at all. Books are simply one media of many different methods of presenting the information.

So that said, let's look at some of the characteristics of the Content Mapping writing system and how the Content Mapping System meets our criteria for efficiently and reliably developing quality learning content in the form of books. By the way, in the rest of this chapter, I'm going to be lazy and refer to the system as CMapping.

Process decomposition

Now the first of the characteristics we wanted was to break the process into a series of small, easy to perform steps. Many systems consist of three steps: outline your book, write your book, edit your book. All the editing in one lump. All the writing in one lump. In fact, some of the systems don't even break it up that far. CMapping breaks each of those tasks out into a set of detailed steps. Each step is unique and focused on a single task and a single output. The full system begins with a marketing objective, followed by a detailed design, structural editing, writing, revising, polishing, and so forth.

The result is a much more effective and efficient method of writing. Specific steps can be (and are) rearranged to eliminate waste and make the process more efficient and effective.

For example, a traditional "write - revise - edit - revise" cycle, places the structural editing at the end when it is difficult and costly to make changes. You end up discarding much of your writing after you've written a number of pages — which end up never being in the final book at all.

The CMapping system, on the other hand, separates the structural editing from both the revision editing and the third party polishing editing.

This allows the structural editing to be placed within the process at the point where revisions are the least expensive in terms of wasted time and energy.

Detailed description of elements

The second characteristic we need to look for is that steps are properly explained or walked through in some way. Tools for the step should be provided or identified. In many ways, this is a result of performing the first characteristic properly. The best illustration of this from CMapping is the use of the Content Map itself to create a detailed, outline at a paragraph level. The tool itself helps you to focus and to develop an outline at the appropriate level of detail. In many systems, the outlining task is described as "Write down the first thing you want to say, then the second and continue to the end." None of which is particularly helpful when you are actually doing it, or converting the outline to an actual book.

Recognition of different variations of tasks

We've already mentioned the best illustration of the recognition of variations on tasks. Specifically, I'm talking about editing. In the traditional writing systems, editing is described as a single monolithic task that occurs at the end of the process. However, the CMapping system identifies three types of editing that matter: structural, revision, and third party polishing. This helps CMapping to prevent writing garbage at all. By doing your structural edit before you begin writing rather than at the end in a lump, you don't write a lot of information that doesn't belong where you're putting it. Or even worse, information that doesn't belong at all.

This segmentation allows CMapping to make the thought processes easier, by focusing on one thought process per step. In a traditional writing system, the writer constructs the summary in a single step. Identifying the information, sequencing it, and editing it in a single activity. In addition, the writing of the book also consists of large, complex lumps. CMapping, however, breaks the process into tiny, single thought process steps. Information is retrieved as a single step within the design sub-process. The Content Map tool helps to organize that information in an automatic way. However, editing and re-organizing the information takes place in separate steps within the design sub-process and the structural edit. Sequencing of the information is a third independent step in the production of the Content Map. Each thought process is kept separate, allowing the brain to work quickly without stopping and restarting. The result is a reduction in the amount of energy and the perceived difficulty when completing this task.

The depth of planning is also a good illustration of this characteristic. Most systems say sit down and do an outline, then write. For example, many systems suggest that a 10 x 10 matrix of topics and questions is the proper way to create an outline. Then they expect you to write a full page of 250 words answering each question. Effectively, they are requiring you to retrieve information, organize it, edit it and present it all as you move from summary to written work. That's why people hate writing.

Isolation of different types of thinking

As we've mentioned CMapping breaks the process down into a series of very specific steps. CMapping starts with a plan or a set of marketing objectives. Designing your book is a separate set of tasks (provided by the tool), as is ordering the result, and the eventual writing and editing. Each step consists of either creation, retrieval of information, organizing information, sequencing, or presenting information. And only one of those activities is performed per step. When you finish the design phase, you have a detailed design at the paragraph level. In fact, it's so detailed that all you need to do is add 100 words to each item in the design. One hundred words is basically an opening sentence, three sentences to develop or illustrate the idea, and one conclusion.

The result is a detailed plan that is easier to use, takes less time to create, and produces a better quality product. And a process that doesn't exhaust you from constant switching between thinking modes.

Use of cognitive tools

The fifth characteristic is rather obvious. We've already discounted lists and matrixes from traditional writing systems as poor solutions. They are not cognitive tools. CMapping is built around the content map as the center of the system. The content map looks like a mind map. It isn't one, but it resembles one. This is because a content map is an extended hybrid Semantic Network Diagram. Mind maps and content maps are related in the same way that a Rolls Royce and a Smart Car are related. They're both cars. That's why the easiest way to teach a content map is to teach mind maps first and then teach the differences and how to use the content map.

Appropriate level of detail

I've already talked about how the CMapping system breaks the book into one-paragraph chunks. You can, of course, break the book into even finer segments (and theoretically less fine segments) if you prefer. So I'm not going to expand on the sixth characteristic any further.

Builds in consistent quality

The final characteristic we are looking for is the inclusion of quality assurance items to ensure that we expend effort only on work that is producing a quality piece of writing. In a traditional writing system, there is little focus on writing only well organized, high quality sections that will be part of the final book. In those systems, an outline is the only real effort made to ensure that a quality book is produced. Most systems don't bother to ask the questions about the reader. For whom are you writing this book? What do they want from your book? What are they expecting? What is my book going to look like? Why am I writing this book? To produce a quality book, you need to know the answer to these questions up front. And you need to be constantly driven by the answers as you design and write the book.

In the CMapping system, quality begins when objectives are separated from the design. Reader's needs are identified up front. But that's not enough. You need to have the answers — the quality rules — in front of you while you are designing. Your design needs to be constantly focused on producing a match to those quality rules. In our case, the content map has the answers in the top half of the form. You are looking at the rules all the time you're designing.

In terms of writing, edits are your major form of quality control. And you need these to be efficient and effective.

Most writing systems have a single defined edit at the end of the writing cycle. In the CMapping system, the structural edit occurs before detailed writing. There is also a separate revision edit during the writing cycle. And finally, there is a third party polishing edit after writing. Each of these edits has a different focus. Each of them checks something different. What the CMapping process does is place an edit at each stage of the process so that all the work is done based on a previous intermediate product that is as good as you can make it. So rework is reduced.

What I have described above are the processes and procedures that you will find within my proprietary writing system, Content Mapping. If you want to discover more about this system you can find my book "How to Write Your Own How-to Book in 24 Hours or Less" on the web at http://www.learningcreators.com/products/buyebook.

As discussed briefly, other writing systems may have a very different approach. This may be because they are looking to support a very different type of writing (e.g. popular entertainment pieces). Or they may have different priorities. Or they just might do things differently. That's cool. The important thing is to have the right characteristics in your system — not that they be implemented the same way.

Choose or develop your writing system carefully. Your success is riding on how consistently and how easily you create good quality writing products!

"I can write anywhere. I made up the names of the characters on a sick bag while I was on an airplane. I told this to a group of kids and a boy said, 'Ah, no, that's disgusting.' And I said, 'Well, I hadn't used the sick bag.'"
- J. K. Rowling

Chapter 5:

Finding Your Own Writing Hole

Systems are more than just process

There is more to any system than just the processes used to create the product. And a writing system is no different. Your writing environment is also critical to your success as a writer, and is a core element in your overall writing system. After all, you wouldn't expect to cut diamonds at a rock concert, or practice heavy metal guitar in a library, would you?

In this chapter, I am going to talk about the second of the three parts that make up a system. More specifically, I'm going to cover:

- Why you need a proper writing environment
- What to look for when finding your environment
- Some practical alternatives and ways to create a personal writing hole that meets your needs

What is a writing hole?

An experienced writer can write anywhere. The important question is, "What can they write?" Quickly followed by, "How productive will they be writing under those conditions?" There is an old saying that a poor worker may make a good system fail, but a good worker will make any system succeed. And writing is no different.

However, if you are having problems finding time to write, you aren't so lucky. As we've already discussed, a quality writing system is critical to finding the time to write. You need a writing system that makes writing easy. Your environment is a key part of your overall writing system. So you need a writing hole that helps you to write.

Finding Your Own Writing Hole

Your writing hole is that little part of the world where you can create an environment that helps you write. A little hole in the wall you can fall down until you reach the source of your imagination. A place of safety from which you can broadcast your deepest thoughts. A place of comfort and discovery. Your own private hobbit hole.

Why call it a writing hole?

Besides the obvious writerly love of metaphor, there is a very specific reason not to call it an office or desk or some such business like term. As you'll discover shortly, every writer is different. What works for one writer won't necessarily work for another. Even one writer may need several writing holes. Not all of those hobbit holes will include the traditional office furniture. If I called it an office or desk, then you would automatically presume that you needed a separate room in your home — or elsewhere. And that simply isn't true.

The second reason is that a hole is traditionally a place to hide. Butch Cassidy and the Sundance Kid would hole up in a cabin near the Hole-in-the-Wall pass. Writing is a solitary activity. Having a place to hide away from interruptions is one of the requirements.

Why have a writing hole?

The next question you need to ask is, "Why?"

Why have a separate writing space? Why have your own little, designated writing hole?

Setting aside an area as your designated "writing place" can be unpopular with your family. It can be difficult to squeeze the space out of a limited living area. And it's almost always expensive to buy the right equipment and furnishings.

Despite these difficulties, not setting an area up where you can write could be the worst mistake you ever make. It could see your dreams of being a successful writer crumble as you struggle to achieve results in an unsupportive environment.

If it's hard to concentrate, you'll avoid writing. Writing requires you to be able to concentrate. Writing is an activity that occurs as much in the intellectual world as it does in the physical world. For most people, being able to concentrate requires several conditions — including limited noise and limited interruptions. Part of the criteria for choosing your writing space is to pick a place that helps you focus on your writing.

Simply finding a place to write is important. If it's hard to find a place to write ... you'll avoid writing. Having a set place means you never have to search around for a quiet area that will work for you. It takes away the guesswork and the effort of having to decide on where you wish to work today.

Having a place to write also takes away the effort involved in gathering the tools of your trade. And believe it or not, a writer does need some tools. If it's hard to get your stuff together ... you'll avoid writing. If you've got a fixed place to write then you can have your writing stuff all laid out and ready for when you choose to write.

Finally, if it takes time to get yourself together ... you'll avoid writing. After all, we all have limited time available. If you get that "gotta write now" feeling, you don't want to lose it. We can't afford to waste our precious minutes. However, if you already have a place prepared — all you have to do is say "I'm going to write now." And you can go write.

Do you sense the theme here? If there's something that gets in the way, it becomes an excuse to avoid writing. By picking and preparing a place to write, you can eliminate many of those excuses to avoid writing.

Writer's Block Demolition

What to look for in a writing hole

So what should you look for in a writing place?

Your designated "writing place" must have the right characteristics to function as an effective writing place. That's fairly straightforward. If it doesn't have the right characteristics, it isn't going to help you write. And it isn't going to eliminate your excuses to write. It may even create some excuses.

The trick is that you need to define what those characteristics mean to you. Each of us is different. And, to make matters worse, we change over time. What works today may not work tomorrow. Perhaps we're tired, or we're stressed out, or we're full of energy, or focused on our writing. We all go through emotional and mental cycles. We all work differently.

Despite the fluid nature of your answers, you'll find there are four major characteristics that you need in a writing hole.

Controllable

You need to be able to exercise control over your writing hole. For example, if you need the room to be neat when you work and your family is constantly leaving the area a mess, a common area isn't going to work as your writing hole. You'll need a specific area just for yourself. Or if you like to work in clutter, having people come in and move things around can ruin the area for you. You won't be able to find things you need when you need them. Your very careful filing system — and that's what a messy desk typically is — will be disrupted.

One aspect of control is most easily expressed as, "You need to be able to shut the door." In this case, I'm really talking about your need to be able to eliminate distractions. Ultimately, you need to be able to control noise in your writing hole. Everyone likes a different level of noise. Everyone defines noise differently. You may be happy with working while playing your music cranked all the way to the top. But someone else's music playing quietly in the background may drive you around the bend. Or you may need absolute quiet. You may even need noise to keep you mentally sharp. You may even find that your definition of noise changes depending on a number of factors. Maybe you're tired one day. Or maybe you're busy. Or maybe you're relaxed and energized. Whatever the situation, you need to have exactly the level of noise you require on that particular day. And that means you must be able to control the level of noise.

The other side of having a door is that you need to know you can walk away and your writing space won't change the next time you go to write. You need to know that if you leave your notes organized on your desk, those notes will still be there in the morning. There you are. You've organized your notes all over your desk. There are little piles representing each section you're writing. Then you walk in the next morning and all those notes are over in the corner of the desk. Or worse, someone tossed your notes in the dustbin because your family didn't realize that the little scraps of paper were important. Now you have to redo everything. Being able to control access to your writing hole is critical — especially for those of us who like to spread ideas out.

One thing to bear in mind is that having a "door" does not necessarily mean that there is a physical door. I bring that up because if you are a freelance writer, you are running a business. And that means that you must declare your income. On the other hand, you get to deduct your expenses from your taxable income. However, in order to deduct your office expenses, your taxation authority may require you to have a separate office with a door. Or you may be able to deduct office expenses because your home represents the sole office area and doors are irrelevant. Your accountant will be able to tell you if you need to worry about that issue. My concern in this book is strictly with a door as it represents your ability to control your workspace.

As you continue along the writer's path, you will inevitably receive suggestions on how to best setup your own writing hole. There are articles on the subject published daily. However, the most important thing you need to remember is that you need your writing space to meet your own requirements. You need to control its characteristics. It needs to match your needs. You need to make it your writing space. There's no point in creating a writing hole that meets someone else's needs. Or one that meets the needs of your accountant or spouse. It needs to meet your own personal needs. This is something that you need to remember whenever you listen to someone's advice on setting up your writing hole. It's your writing hole, not theirs. You do not, and will not, work the same way as they do. There are no absolutes — and no advice that meets everyone's needs.

Available

Your writing hole has to be available on your schedule ... not everyone else's. We all have a circadian rhythm, a time of day where we are most effective for particular types of work. It will vary from person to person although it tends to follow particular patterns. Even on a weekly pattern, we have certain days that are more conducive to writing. For example, I work in the living room — great during the day not so hot after the kids come home around three. But that's cool because I do most of my writing in the morning. The rest of the day I can work anywhere under almost any conditions. Besides, if the kids are home on a school holiday I always have my formal office if I need to disappear. And the pool ... and the music room ... and even the basement if I'm desperate.

A second variation on the availability theme is the need to start writing immediately. You need to have everything at hand so can start writing as soon as you have time available. You have to be able to just sit down, pick up your stuff, and start writing. Otherwise, as I mentioned earlier, you'll use the delay to avoid writing. Not to mention that you'll waste precious minutes preparing instead of doing. The key is to be able to open it up and start immediately. If you're sharing the area, you may not be able to start without having to spend time to prepare your writing space. There are always ways to get around sharing but however you set up your writing hole, you need be able to start without any delay.

One modern life comment is that physical space isn't always required. For example, you could have everything you need on a USB memory stick. Find a computer and plug in the stick and you're ready to go.

Private

I've covered several of the aspects of privacy in the discussion on control. After all, privacy is one of the key reasons that you need to control your space. It stands to reason that many of the aspects are common. But there are some specific aspects that are unique to privacy as a characteristic.

One of those aspects is the need to be able to be a little silly. After all, sometimes as a writer you need to act out scenes. Even non-fiction writers occasionally need to think things out verbally. After all, writing is just speaking on paper. How your words sound is important. And thinking aloud can be a little embarrassing if you are doing it in front of an audience. People tend to look at you a little strangely when you're pacing around the room and talking to yourself. Imagine the strange looks you would get if you were caught playing out a love scene — by yourself. Or a murder scene. Imagine how you would feel explaining to your police department's rapid response team that you were all alone and you hadn't really flushed a body down the toilet. Or that pistol you were threatening someone with was a toy, and the person you were threatening was imaginary.

Of course, thinking aloud isn't the only noise that comes from a writer's hole. Writing is frustrating from time to time. And every writer feels the occasional need to be able to express his or her

Writer's Block Demolition

feelings. And while four letter words have been in common use since before English was English, they aren't generally accepted in polite company. Sometimes you don't want anyone else to observe you while you're swearing your fool head off. Especially if you have young children that you would prefer not learn "those words" quite yet.

Under the control heading, I discussed the need to be able to close things up and leave it, knowing that no one would disturb your work. The example and focus I used had to do with controlling disruptions. But there is another aspect that is directly related to privacy.

You need to be able to leave notes out and know that someone else isn't going to read those notes. You have no idea how much trouble someone reading your unfinished book can cause. A long time ago, before I wrecked my leg, I wrote fiction. I've written fiction for as long as I can remember. One of the stories I wrote, had to do with someone having anger issues. It was basically a murder mystery piece. I had many notes related to anger and frustration with co-workers in which I expressed some very negative emotions. Unfortunately, my girlfriend at the time found them and read them. It took me a long time to convince her that these weren't my emotions. I was just writing about a character. Yes, they were based on my emotions. But the reactions and the focus were entirely wrong. I wasn't angry with my co-workers. I didn't hate my job (in fact, I loved my job at the time). And no, I wasn't about to kill anyone. Not my style. I don't do those kinds of things. Even to editors — no matter how much I might want to. No matter how many excuses they might give me.

Spacious

I had a problem naming this characteristic. In North America, we've somehow turned spacious and big into synonyms. But the root of spacious is space. Spacious simply means more than enough room. It's slightly larger than ample, but much less than overwhelming. Bluntly put, spacious means enough space to hold your crap plus a little bit more. Not someone else's crap — your crap. If you only have a chair, a six by six room would be spacious. The definition of what is spacious will change depending on what you are talking about. And the definition can also change based on whom you're talking about.

For a writer that means you need to identify your definition of space up front.

In the case of software, you're talking about hard disk space. In the case of web access, it's bandwidth plan and speed or type of access. In the case of your desk, it's room to write & hold references. In the case of your library, do you have enough bookshelves to hold all your books? Okay, so that last one is an oxymoron, there's never enough space to hold your books.

It could be as simple as do you have enough wall space to put up your storyboard and storymaps and other types of notes.

Once you've determined the type of space that matters the physical definition of spacious is entirely up to you. That's the only person to whom it matters. It can be as small as a little book. In my case, I use a small notebook for all my notes. All I need is a spare pocket to shove the book into. I find it more convenient than a computer. On the other hand, I've known writers that have needed four walls and a whole office to hold their writing stuff. You need to decide what enough space means for you.

Sometimes I need

As I've said several times so far, every writer is different and every day is different. I can't tell you what you need and be honest with you. My way is not your way. That's why the advice books so often fail. They don't acknowledge the differences between people and instead attempt to impose one solution on everyone.

And that means it's time for you to make some decisions.

Finding Your Own Writing Hole

I suggest that you start with a blank piece of paper. Give yourself a bit of space for column headings, and then draw three columns on the paper. The outer two should be wide, while the inner column only needs to hold a single seven-letter word. At the top of the first column, you are going to write the heading, "Sometimes when ... ". At the top of the third column, you are going to write the phrase, "my writing space needs". In the middle you need to list the words "Control, When, Privacy, Size".

Begin with a situation — for example, "I am writing at home to a deadline." This goes in the first column under the "Sometimes when ..." heading. In the second column, put the word "Control".

In the third column, describe how much control and what type of control you will need over your writing hole if you were writing at home to a deadline.

Leave a little room, and then enter the word "When" in the second column. In the third column, describe when you will be writing at home to a deadline. Is it in the morning? Is it all day? What other conditions might exist at that time? Will anyone else be home?

Leave a little room and then go on to privacy. Put the word "Privacy" in the second column and describe your privacy needs in the third. Do the same for "Size". How much room will you need? What will you need to have in your writing hole?

Finally draw a line across all three columns and then go on to the next situation. Continue doing this until you've defined your needs in all the situations you can think of. When you finish, you'll have a list of the characteristics that each of your writing holes will need. All you have to do now is find a writing hole that meets those criteria for each of those situations.

Finding your writing hole

So far in this chapter, I have looked at the importance of creating the appropriate writing environment, and the critical role played by the place you choose as your writing hole. I've also described a set of characteristics for you to identify what you need in your writing space. And hopefully, you've taken the time to actually develop the criteria to identify your writing hole.

Now it's time to put that information into practice. It's time to find your writing space.

So where can you find your writing hole? Or two or three.

Finding Your Own Writing Hole

There's no rule saying you can only have one. In fact, you may find that having two or more provides you the flexibility to meet all the criteria whereas having one might not meet all the criteria and situations.

No matter how many writings holes you have, you need to have at least one writing hole of your own. A place that gives you the freedom to open up and start writing immediately. A place where you have all your writing gear to hand. A place with your computer, your pens, your pads, your dictionary, your thesaurus. Everything you need to write, immediately available.

So where should you look?

You could use a traditional office. You can rent office space. After all, you are a business when you are writing. Why not run it like a business? Now reality check — renting a proper office can be expensive and it defeats the purpose of being a home business. But it's much less expensive than not writing at all. And not everyone works best from their home. So it might be the best solution for you. Or if you don't want to lease or rent an office — or can't justify the expense — there are always hoteling services. These are shared offices where you rent the space by the hour or by the day. Often these services provide other facilities such as answering services, a boardroom, and secretarial services.

Writer's Block Demolition

Of course, you don't have to have a traditional office. You can always set up an office at home.

You could convert a back bedroom. In fact, some newer homes have an office space built in, complete with wiring for a second phone line and facilities for many other services.

You can use the area under the stairs or in a closet. If you have an unfinished staircase — a stair with nothing underneath — you can convert that to hold a desk and bookshelves. Or take an unused closet and put a built-in desk and bookshelves in there.

You can even use an armoire or drop front desk. There are desks — complete offices actually — that fit inside a cabinet. These offices-in-a-box are useable almost anywhere. I use one in my living room. Open it up and I've got my desk, my computer, shelves, filing. Everything I need. Close it up and it just looks like a piece of high-end furniture. The workspace disappears.

The armoire looks clean. It leaves the living room uncluttered. And as long as you leave the doors closed no one knows that your desk is about to collapse under the weight of everything you're working on at the moment! Just don't open up the doors quickly! And occasionally purge the mess.

Finding Your Own Writing Hole

If your living room is large enough, modern decorating style is to place a desk in the living room. I presume this is an admission that working from home is part of the modern culture. However, personally I find that an open desk in the living areas tends to become cluttered quickly. But of course, your mileage may vary. Your family may always immediately put things away in their proper places. In which case, this solution might be perfect for you.

The ultimate in simplicity, however, is the briefcase. "Have Briefcase Will Write" is my motto. Personally, I actually use a backpack. But the idea is the same. Everything you need to write is kept in the backpack, ready to go with you. Just grab and go. Your office becomes the nearest Starbucks, or the Library, or even the woods.

Many libraries offer quiet study spaces. Often these are set up with WiFi, or occasionally wired internet access, workstations and power outlets — just as you would find in a modern office. One advantage is that if you identify the need to do some research to support your writing, all the resources of the library are at your disposal. You may have to pre-book to use the space but there is usually no cost involved, and often no restriction on how often you can use the library facility or for how long. The library truly can be an office away from home — a calm and quiet environment where the phone is not constantly disturbing you with its ringing!

Up-market coffee shops such as Starbucks are now also providing a space to work. Even Tim Hortons is now in the game. These coffee shops also provide WiFi — usually for free. And they are comfortable with small business people and home workers camping out in their facilities for extended periods. They even tolerate writers. Of course, there is a certain set of unwritten rules involved. But coffee shops do make a comfortable place to work. And you can get a coffee or tea too!

Of course, if you're really hungry — even McDonalds is now providing free WiFi and encouraging business people to hang around.

But those are not the only places you can use.

With the advent of internet sticks, you can take your WiFi connection with you just about anywhere. When I was in university, we had a forest on the campus. So whenever I wanted to work in a quiet area I'd grab a blanket and my backpack and tramp off into the woods. Find a tree and a comfortable spot and I was all set. It was comfortable, quiet and private. The only noise was bird song. And as for privacy, other than the occasional chipmunk with an overly developed sense of curiosity, I seldom saw a living thing. It was a great place to work.

Of course, this was long before the internet — when electricity wasn't mandatory for writing. But with tablets and netbooks and notebooks and internet sticks — well, having a tether isn't a necessity. At least not as long as you've charged up your batteries well before you head out.

An effective, comfortable, and safe writing place can result in a dramatic reduction in your frustration level, and create opportunities for creativity and breakthroughs. You deserve an environment that supports the achievement of your goals, and provides a tranquil relief from the stormy seas of conflicting demands on your time.

"Amateurs sit and wait for inspiration, the rest of us just get up and go to work."
— Stephen King, On Writing

"Cats are dangerous companions for writers because cat watching is a near-perfect method of writing avoidance"
— Dan Greenburg

Chapter 6:

It's All In the Wrist

The third of three

The process you use to work and the environment in which you work are important. But there are three parts to the systems equation. Process, environment, and agent. The agent in this case being you. All three come together to turn effort into results. The third part of the equation is you and *how* you work.

There are a lot of good work habits that you need to encourage. Ones that increase your ability to be motivated, to keep productive, and to have success in your professional writing.

And there are a lot of bad habits.

The YOU in the system

I've said before that I prefer dealing with problems holistically. So if I'm going to deal with the agent part of a system, then I need to deal with all of the agent part. ("Agent" is the process analyst term for you). Unlike, process and environment, there are two characteristics of the agent that affect the overall system. Specifically, what the agent brings to the mix and how the agent applies those skills. In other words, for our purposes how good a writer you are and your work habits.

In this chapter, I'm going to focus on the application portion. You are you and I'm not trying to change you. My interest is in helping you to get more done. So I'm going to deal with the "your contribution" portion very quickly so that I can move on to your work habits.

However, don't base your opinion of the importance of this on my emphasis (or lack of emphasis) on this topic. I'm not focused on helping you to become a better writer — just more prolific. That doesn't mean it isn't important that you write well. Only that I'm not here for that purpose.

It's All In The Wrist

It's easy for people to say that anyone can write a book. Worse, it's easy for people to believe that even if they won't say it aloud. That's why writers are traditionally underpaid.

The truth is that writing is a craft. It is not an easy craft by any means. And it does not come naturally. It is, however, a craft that anyone can develop skills in. If they are willing to put in the effort to learn the craft, anyone can write a book. The tools to write a book can be learned. However, not everyone is willing to put in the effort required. And frankly, not everyone should.

However, don't let this stop or frighten you. If you wish to write, you can do so. There are four basic things that you need to do to build your skill in the craft.

The first is to read. Read everything. Read anything. Read all things. Read the backs of cereal boxes. Read the fronts of cereal boxes. Read popular fiction. Read classical fiction. Read genre fiction. Read non-fiction. One of the worst pieces of advice I have ever heard came from Stephen R. Covey. He recommended that you avoid popular fiction and read only the classics. That is a big mistake. Today's readers are not yesterday's readers. You need to read everything to be able to understand what makes a classic touch people long after their time. And that includes mistakes that should never have seen the printed page.

Read voraciously, but most of all, read actively. What do I mean by read actively? As you read, ask yourself, "Is this working?" Does it engage your interest? Does it hook you into its story? But don't stop there. Why and how must follow if you wish to learn. What is the writer doing to hook you in? Why does that work? And always ask yourself, "How could I have done it better?"

Of course, if you are going to critique the masters, you need to know how to write yourself. So spend time learning the building blocks of your craft. Collect words. Words are your raw materials. Keep a dictionary and thesaurus on your smartphone and use them frequently. Read the style manuals such as the APA Style Guide, the Chicago Manual of Style or The Canadian Style. Sentences are the melody of your craft. Learn how to construct a sentence properly and how to format the pieces and parts.

Once you've learned how to write and studied others at their craft, you need to apply your knowledge. That's how you internalize your learning. So practice writing. Write consistently. Write constantly. Write anything. Don't worry about your genre. Don't worry about the subject. Don't worry about keeping it. Don't worry about using it. A single paragraph at a time is sufficient. Just do it often. Then put the piece away and come back to it in a month's time. Forget the typos and the spelling mistakes. How could you have done it better? How could you have made it tighter, more moving, more effective?

The fourth and final activity is to trust yourself. You are no longer in school. You have a voice that you've developed on the street, in your living room, in your office, in your life. It is part of who you are. Trust it. In the second activity, you learned the rules of writing. And hopefully you learned the "why" behind those rules. But always remember two things.

The first is that most of the rules aren't really rules at all. Many of the rules were developed by a teacher in Victorian London. He made them up from whole cloth to fit his prejudices. A trait for which the Victorians were famous. For example, you've been taught in school that split infinitives are not proper English (not to too quickly pick a second example such as "To boldly go"). In Latin, split infinitives are not correct. In fact, they aren't actually possible. However, English is not a Romance Language. Split infinitives are perfectly acceptable in English and its antecedents. Despite the desires of that Victorian London teacher and generations of teachers since then, we do not speak Latin. Sorry. The grammar rules of English are different from the grammar rules of Latin. As Raymond Chandler wrote, "When I split an infinitive, God damn it, I split it so it will stay split."

The second is that people want to connect with you, the writer. If you write fiction, they want to connect with your characters certainly. But they need to connect with the storyteller. They need to touch you as a person. Otherwise, they will not be touched by what you write. And one of the ways they touch you is by hearing **you** speak. By hearing the you — your voice — behind the ideas you promote. Your voice, your natural way of speaking, needs to shine through. Formal writing is for school. And frequently it is used to justify bad writing. Write as you speak. Even if you later have to clean it up, you will be further ahead.

Your job as a writer is first, last and always to communicate. Your words, your sentences, and your grammar are your tools. How you use those tools defines your ability as a writer. But how well you communicate with those tools defines your success as a writer. It's not the hammer, and it's not the wood. It's the beauty of the panel and the smoothness of the sliding drawer that matters.

Work habits

Now that we've cleared the air about your basic abilities, how do we get the most from those abilities? That's the purpose of work habits. Work habits are simply a set of habits that you need to develop in order to get the most from your efforts. It's how you work on whatever process you choose.

For our purposes, there are three basic types of good habits:

1. Be kind to your body
2. Take breaks
3. Create writing rituals

This topic is so important that I'm going to deal with each of these in their own section in this chapter.

Be kind to your body

There is a belief that writing is an intellectual exercise. And to a certain extent, it is. But it is also a physical exercise. Your mind is an organ. It is part of your body. Its effectiveness depends on the state of your body. So you need to keep your body in good shape in order to support your mind.

The problem of course, is that writing is also a sedentary and physically damaging activity.

To overcome the effects of this you need to do three things. You need to eat properly. You need to exercise. And you need to get the proper amount of sleep.

Writer's Block Demolition

Eat properly

The body is a machine. In order to function it must have the right fuel. If you want to write well you need good & proper food. If you don't supply your body with the proper food, it's going to stop working for you. Unfortunately, as writers we tend to fill our mouths with the wrong food in a snatch and grab manner. And our waistlines tend to display that fact for the world to see. We need to change our habits.

The first change is to change our snacking habits. Snack on carrots, celery, and other vegetables. Use fresh fruit for a quick energy boost when you need it. Don't snack on candy, chocolates, or high sugar dried fruit. My favorite, personally, is the snack bar. Bad move. Like most writers, I need to watch the calories and those snack bars have almost a day's worth of calories in a single bar. They are deadly. Thirty pounds later, I can guarantee that you don't want to snack on snack bars. No matter what your taste buds think.

You also need to watch the amount of caffeine you ingest. Most writers like to drink coffee or tea while they're writing. In fact, it's a running joke that writers' fuel is coffee. Tea isn't too bad but coffee is a killer. Unless it's decaffeinated and I don't consider that real coffee. Try to limit it to only one in the morning. Your body will be much happier with you than if it's trying to deal with the shakes from a dozen coffees a day. And your writing will also be less shaky. Scary thing is I used to be a heavy coffee drinker. In fact, I used to drink espressos at two in the morning just before heading to bed. Now that I've cut back, I can feel my heart pressure rising when I've had too many cups.

At the risk of showing my British ancestry — try tea instead. Seriously. Better still have a tisane. Many herbal teas will provide the throat softening and relaxation without any caffeine. (Not all herbal teas are caffeine free, so read the label). Just don't let my wife hear this — my response to herbal is a consistent "No thanks." I like milk and sugar in my tea and in fact, I prefer for the spoon to stand up in my cuppa. But at least I admit that I'm being bad.

Related to this is the need to watch your hydration. Again, one of the problems with drinking coffee or tea is that they are diuretics. You need to make sure you are drinking enough pure liquid — water being the most obvious. If you're on a roll with your writing, you're not going to want to get up and get a drink. If you're anything like me, you could easily find yourself not getting any liquid into you at all for days at a time.

At the risk of being the pot in this exchange, part of eating properly is to watch your weight. As a writer, you're going to spend a lot of time sitting. That can lead to blood clots in the legs. Especially if your weight is up. As you get heavier, sitting gets more and more difficult. And writing becomes more and more difficult. Not only that but getting that weight off again becomes even more and more difficult. So you need to watch your weight closely. If you notice your belt becoming tighter it's probably too late. You need to deal with the issue of body weight on a regular basis and adjust your eating habits if you begin to grow.

Exercise

An alternative to adjusting your eating habits if you start gaining weight is to increase the exercise you get. Even if you are skinny as a rail and never need to diet, you will need to include exercise in your daily routine. As I said previously, writing isn't a particularly active sport. You are sitting in a chair all day long, pounding at a keyboard using movements that are guaranteed to damage your hands and wrists. And most likely in a position that will damage your back and neck.

The food that you are consuming is energy. If it is not being used it will be stored. Around your waist as fat being the most obvious method. Your brain needs energy to perform. You need energy to write. If the energy is stored as fat, your brain will be starved when it comes time to feed it energy. You could avoid eating (i.e. diet) but the body also needs the nutrients in the food. If you don't eat properly, you won't get those nutrients. Exercise helps your body to burn the excess energy and to keep the energy that remains available to the body quickly while keeping the nutrients high. And that includes for non-physical activities such as writing and thinking.

To overcome the storage issue, the low metabolism issue, and the physical damage issues, you need to include an exercise regimen in your daily writing.

We all think of exercise in a traditional, get away from the desk format. For example, you can get up from the desk and go for a walk. You could go for a run if you're up for it. Or play racquetball or squash or cricket or baseball or basketball or hockey. There are a million and one ways to relax, have fun, and burn calories.

But away from the desk isn't the only place you can exercise. You can do stretching exercises at your desk. You can do resistance exercises. There are devices such as stationary bicycles that can be used. Some even fit under the desk. Even a simple barbell can be a source of exercise while editing your book.

Just remember that being away from your desk for a period of time is an important factor in your overall health.

Sleep

Most writers have a problem. When they are on a roll, they don't stop. They are so focused on their writing that they lose track of time and everything else around them. I know that I — and every writer I know — has had at least one all night writing episode. You know the ones where you look up and suddenly realize that's the sun coming in the window of your writing hole. Or you blink and it's suddenly four in the morning and you have to be up at six.

The sad truth is you can't work all the time. And to produce reasonable quantities of quality writing you need to get plenty of sleep. Otherwise, your productivity is going to drop. You're going to have problems thinking. You're going to fall asleep while you are writing. You're going to get tired and you're not going to be able to work well.

Not only that but your family is going to get upset with you and your emotional health will suffer.

The quality and amount of your writing isn't the only issue when you fail to get enough sleep.

Sleep is where the body repairs itself. During your sleep periods, the muscles and organs are free to focus energy on repairs. Tiny tears that occur during activity are repaired while the muscles are dormant. Nerve ending are rebuilt and synapses are restored. That's why doctors linked fibromyalgia and sleep deprivation for so long. Fibromyalgia causes sleeplessness and without the sleep to repair the nerve endings, the Fibromyalgia gets worse. The result is an ever-worsening cycle.

Sleep is also where mind repairs and resets itself. Without sleep, especially REM, the brain becomes overloaded. Problems become worse and fears grow. Temper becomes shorter and numerous mental problems begin to show. And yes, this is personal experience talking.

You see, the mind doesn't actually shut down during sleep. It simply stops trying to forcing itself into patterns you have chosen. That's why your dreams are often so disjointed and strange. And also, why you may go to bed and wake up having the answer to a problem. Sleep is when the brain reviews what has happened during the day and shuffles memories into their proper order. It's where the brain begins to make sense of what it observed and feared during the day.

Sleep allows you to make connections that you never knew existed. It allows your brain to process and link ideas and concepts and activities with those that have already been stored. It allows you to find patterns that the waking mind was too busy to identify.

Take breaks (not just sleep)

Sufficient sleep once a day isn't the whole answer, however. You also need to take breaks from your writing for reasons other than sleep. It sounds counter-productive but it really isn't. If you overwork yourself, you will find yourself becoming less productive. The more time you put in, the less work you accomplish in that time. In fact, after a certain point the effect begins to reduce the total work accomplished. Breaks help us to retain our productivity and therefore are important to our overall productivity.

Working at a computer (or notebook) is hard on the body. You have a glare from the screen (or paper) that is hard on the eyes. You are sitting in a chair for long periods, compressing parts of the body that aren't meant to be compressed. You are using muscles for long periods that aren't meant to be used for long periods. You are subjecting bones to impacts that the body isn't designed to receive and ignore.

Occupational therapists say work for 45 minutes then take a 15-minute break to walk and stare out the window. Your body, eyes, and mind need the rest. Your eyes need to cycle through various focus lengths (near, medium and far). A computer screen is typically a very short focus length so you should look at something far away in order to rest your eyes. Your muscles also need to try other configurations. Muscles that are tensed need to relax. Muscles that are relaxed need to tense. Moving around will help to ensure that your body doesn't lock in a particular combination of tense and relaxed muscles. Trust me it hurts when that happens.

Taking a break also gives you a chance to recover the energy you are expending in concentration and mental effort. It gives you a chance to let the muscle at the top of your spinal column relax and go off in other directions.

The problem of course, is that it is much harder to do than to say. Especially when you're on a roll and the writing is coming fast and easy. I know with myself that when I'm on a roll I really don't want to stop. It's just type, type, type until I can't see and my fingers are ready to fall off. There are times when I can't even stand up after a marathon session. (Okay, I have problems doing that at the best of times. It's just worse when I'm working for too long.) And when I'm writing a book, I'm usually okay for the week but the next week I can barely move.

And that's not a good thing!

Along that same idea, you need to keep regular hours if possible. You'll find that keeping regular hours will make your life much simpler and improve your life balance. There's a tendency when working from home to work all day and all night. The problem is that you are driving your life out of balance that way. There's more to life than just working — even if it is writing. You need time for your family. You need time for yourself. You can't work all the time. And if you want to keep your relationships you need to spend time working on them. So keep a limit on the hours you spend with your writing.

Do you ever get into a massive writing campaign? You know those weeks and weeks of writing every minute of the day. Take a short break and recharge the batteries. That weekend off will actually help increase your productivity. I regularly produce between 200 and 300 articles in a 100-day period. At the end of that period, I need to take a week or so and not write. Maybe I'll go off and create a course. Or I'll write on a completely different subject. Or I'll do something totally unrelated. This dead period helps me to recover and then produce even more when I go back to writing.

Create writing rituals

Sounds silly and kind of new age. But creating a routine or habit that supports writing is important to finding the time to write.

Rituals are one way to build habits. They are just things that we do the same way, every time in order to make sure that we do everything we have to do, or to prepare ourselves mentally for the activity of writing.

For example, maintaining regular hours is one form of a ritual or habit. Maintaining regular hours helps get the work done because you learn to focus on work during that time. Regular hours also help to prevent burnout by limiting the amount of time spent writing. Regular hours also help to prevent family tensions by avoiding an unbalanced emphasis on work.

But of course, rituals don't have to be as massive as maintaining regular hours. They can be as simple as performing a meditation immediately prior to writing or first thing in the morning. Rituals such as this work to relieve stress and help to prevent burnout.

Other rituals may help you get the mind ready to write. These can be very simple things like setting up your computer or preparing your desk. They all work by becoming linked with writing. They are a key to tell your brain to go into writing mode.

"Writing is easy: All you do is sit staring at a blank sheet of paper until drops of blood form on your forehead."
- Gene Fowler

"There's no such thing as writer's block. That was invented by people in California who couldn't write."
― **Terry Pratchett**

"I suspect that writer's block afflicts mainly people who have some stable and ample source of income outside of writing. So far, it hasn't been a problem."
― **Fred Saberhagen**

"Writer's block...a lot of howling nonsense would be avoided if, in every sentence containing the word WRITER, that word was taken out and the word PLUMBER substituted; and the result examined for the sense it makes. Do plumbers get plumber's block? What would you think of a plumber who used that as an excuse not to do any work that day?"
― **Philip Pullman**

Chapter 7:

Turning off Writers Block

The three causes of writer's block

One of the problems with deciding to start every chapter with a quotation from a famous writer illustrating the point of the chapter is picking just

Writer's Block Demolition

one quote. Especially when you get to the chapter on writer's block. You'll notice that I failed spectacularly. Every writer has experienced writer's block at some point in his or her career. And most of them have groused about it at one point or another. Whether it is a matter of rejecting it or describing it, writers are in love with talking about writer's block.

The truth is that writer's block is a fallacy. It doesn't exist. As Philip Pullman the author of 'The Golden Compass' wrote:

"The fact is that writing is hard work, and sometimes you don't want to do it, and you can't think of what to write next, and you're fed up with the whole damn business. Do you think plumbers don't feel like that about their work from time to time? Of course there will be days when the stuff is not flowing freely. What you do then is MAKE IT UP. I like the reply of the composer Shostakovich to a student who complained that he couldn't find a theme for his second movement. "Never mind the theme! Just write the movement!" he said.

Writer's block is a condition that affects amateurs and people who aren't serious about writing. So is the opposite, namely inspiration, which amateurs are also very fond of. Putting it another way: a professional writer is someone who writes just as well when they're not inspired as when they are."

What we perceive as writer's block is actually a matter of three factors coming together and failing at the same time.

One factor is really the point of the previous three chapters. If you have a good writing system then you won't have a problem with writer's block.

Your writing system should include steps that aid you in selecting a topic for your book. And in determining what to write at any point in time. Why? Because your writing system needs to help you write a book that will be purchased and read. And part of that process is to identify what topics your readers will want to read about. Ergo you have a topic. Now all you have to do is go off, put one word after another, and write about the topic. Again, your writing system will help you to determine what those words should be and what order to put them into. So true writer's block, when it occurs, is a symptom of a breakdown in the system you are using to write.

The second factor is the opposite of the other of our keys to finding the time to write. And truth to tell, it is the main reason for writer's block occurring. If motivation is a key to being able to write, demotivation is a force to prevent us from writing. Generally speaking, demotivation occurs when writing becomes linked with a bad result. That's why writer's block is so insidious. And why writing rituals are so important. Effectively you have created a ritual which promotes failure. Maybe writing has been difficult. Or has caused you a great deal of stress. The result is that you will avoid writing. You have associated writing with pain. And we all know that we avoid pain. The solution then is twofold. First, increase our motivation to overcome the demotivator. And second, create a writing ritual that breaks the previous link between writing and pain.

As you can see, if you use the knowledge that this book has given you then (so-called) "writer's block" will not be a problem for you in almost all cases. Motivation and system will typically overcome almost all the issues that may block your writing. If you use the knowledge you have learned so far to find your own writing system and to find your own motivation, then you will overcome ninety percent of all the issues known collectively as "writer's block".

But there still remains the third factor that causes so-called writer's block.

I'm therefore going to focus this chapter on eliminating this third factor from any consideration. If you have already followed the previous information in this book, the first two factors are no longer an issue. Your writing system has cleared the way to eliminate writer's block. You are motivated to overcome anything in your path. So you almost never experience so-called writer's block. And you have created a ritual of writing success that breaks the habit of failure. This further reduces the number of occasions where writing is an unassailable effort. All that's needed to totally eliminate writer's block is this third factor.

The third factor

So what is the third factor?

It's the finding of ideas. It's usually called creativity. And as far as I'm concerned, it is all nonsense (at least for a writer). In fact, solving this issue should be built into your writing system. It's part of the market planning for your book. For a writer creativity is really the identification of ideas that already exist. To use Edward De Bono's terminology, creativity for the writer is less about lateral thinking or thinking out of the box, as it is about vertical thinking or developing ideas through analysis. While lateral thinking is the purview of creativity, vertical thinking is the result of analytical processes.

> "Ideas are like rabbits. You get a couple and learn how to handle them, and pretty soon you have a dozen."
> **— John Steinbeck**

Ideas are all around you. They are in the street. In the market. In the newspaper and on the television and radio. Ideas are not the problem. Finding ideas is not the problem. They are everywhere. Their fecal pellets are piled high in the shops and bookstores.

The problem is to open yourself up to those ideas. To become aware of and willing to acknowledge those ideas. Because humans normally try to avoid ideas — they're dangerous. They lead to change and disruption. And we fear them. We stick our ostrich heads in the ground and pretend they don't exist.

Fortunately, once we overcome our fear and open ourselves up to ideas, we'll find they truly are rabbits in the lettuce patch. In fact, you'll find far more ideas than you can ever explore. Just keeping track of them will become the problem. Closely followed by the need to prioritize and identify those you are going to explore in your writing, rather than those you merely wish to view briefly in passing. That little stream of ideas you wanted? Be warned, it's really a tsunami.

One way to catch the rabbit

There are a number of ways to begin the process. And each form of writing will have its own variations. One technique is simply to begin with the local library. There is a publication called Publisher's Weekly which lists the top selling books and which books are being sold at the moment. There are also a number of other versions of these lists such as the New York Times Bestsellers list. Amazon.com and other booksellers also provide a number of similar lists. Look for trends and identify those topics that are selling well. Then pick those best-selling topics that are of interest. After all, you don't want to waste your time doing something that you hate.

Now that you have your general topic, it's time to flesh the idea out. It's time to read a little in your chosen topic. Go out to the bookstore and library. Find magazines on your topic. What you are hoping to do for non-fiction is to identify what problems readers are experiencing. In the case of fiction, you are hoping to identify ideas, themes, and settings that readers are interested in. Letters to the editor and "Ask the editor" columns are great sources of these ideas. The next source you need to investigate is the internet. Forums, blogs and social media are great places to find the modern equivalents. Travel to conventions and trade shows and bookstores. Get out and talk to the potential readers of your book.

I suggest using a small, leather book to track the ideas you find. For example, Moleskine manufactures a line of notebooks that are perfect for the writer. Leather bound, they will fit into your shirt pocket and survive every day mishaps. Larger versions are also available which fit in a purse or backpack. Personally, I like using the 4 x 6 version. This fits into my portfolios, backpacks, and briefcases. It will even fit into my breast pocket in a pinch. However, there is enough room for my rather wide fingers to make notes comfortably. Unfortunately, if you fill up as many journals as I do, the price for a genuine Moleskine journal may be painful. If you check out the dollar stores, you can find versions that sell for two or three dollars. These journals work just as well even if they aren't as ego boosting.

Once you find the idea you want to explore it's time to brainstorm. I use a tool called the Topic Map. Again, it is a hybrid Semantic Network

Diagram. A mindmap will also work. But brainstorming to a list is almost as effective. (Lists aren't cognitive tools but brainstorming is). Just remember not to edit as you go. Let the ideas flow and bounce from each other. One idea will lead to another and another and so on. It may be helpful to involve other people. Their responses will often help you to release your own ideas. You may also find using a recording device may help by delaying the time spent writing.

Now that you have a list of ideas, it's just a matter of identifying the one that most attracts you. Your writing system should help you to expand on that idea and develop an outline for the book. Once your outline is at the paragraph level, you're ready to write.

You'll find that after a few sessions, you'll be seeing new ideas everywhere. You'll wonder why you ever had any problem finding ideas. It's not that the ideas are new or that they suddenly appear. It's just that you've opened up your mind to seeing and accepting them for what they are.

I should also mention that creative idea generation is not a standalone process. At various stages during the process, you will want to check the marketability of your ideas. There is no point in writing a book — no matter how well written — if no one is going to read it. You must have a market for the idea that forms the seed for your book. Just because you discovered a problem does not automatically imply that people are willing to spend money to solve that problem.

"If you don't have time to read, you don't have the time (or the tools) to write. Simple as that."
— **Stephen King**

Chapter 8:

Defeating the Thieves of Time

Finding the time

So far, I've talked about making the process of making writing easier and I've talked about making sure that your desire to write allows you to overcome the problems you encounter. I've even talked about the role of your writing hole and how it supports your success. As do your work habits.

Now I'm going to talk about the practicalities of finding the time to write. I'm going to go through some ideas to help you actually find minutes during your day to write. This happens to be the chapter that most writers on finding time focus on. However, do not underestimate the importance of all of the prior sections. Without taking into account your motivation, your system, your environment, and your work habits, you'll never get this section to succeed. That's why you haven't had success with all the time management ideas you've had thrown at you before. Unless you deal with all the factors, you won't succeed in finding time to write.

In this chapter, I'm going to talk about some of the problems you may encounter. Why do you lose time? What is it that is preventing you from writing? I'm also going to talk about some of the practicalities in finding those few stolen minutes. And I'm going to show you some of the ways that you can get time back. I'll talk about the three major things that steal your time. And finally, I'm going to look at the solutions to each of those time thieves.

Why we lose time

So far, I've talked about making the process of writing easier. I've also talked about making sure that your desire to write allows you to overcome the problems that you will inevitably encounter. At this point, you should be fired up to write and finding writing to be an efficient, enjoyable process. Now I'm going to look at the practicalities of squeezing those few precious hours out of your very busy day.

So why do we lose writing time?

Why don't we just sit down and write?

Remember I said earlier, "Anyone can write a book". And that control is in your hands.

There are three main reasons that we don't just sit down and write our book:

- Avoidance
- Interruptions
- Time conflicts

Avoidance is just a fancy way of saying that we don't want to write. We find other things to do. We sit there and stare at empty pages. In short, because writing is so hard we do everything in our power to avoid working that hard. The key to solving the problem of avoidance is simply to make writing easier.

Interruptions are the time grabbers, the time thieves. Welcome to modern life. These are all those little, niggly, pain in the neck, irritating disruptions to our concentration. Writing needs the ability to focus. It needs us to be able to concentrate and not keep changing our horse every five seconds. Modern life tries to prevent us from focusing on anything for too long. The solution to interruptions is to eliminate the biggest time wasters.

Writer's Block Demolition

Welcome to modern life. We're all overcommitted. We are all trying to do too much in too little time. We have time conflicts. Or more correctly (non) scheduling issues. There is always something more pressing. Something we absolutely, positively must do now! Not in ten minutes. Now! The key to this last problem is in the title of this book ... find the time. Decide what is less pressing and do your writing instead.

Reducing avoidance

Let's look at the first of the time killers, avoidance. We may not be deliberately avoiding doing that writing project due on Friday. It may be that looking through last month's receipts for the one we need in order to return a pair of socks is *really* more important. Or that pile of laundry really, absolutely must get sorted right this second. Or there is that light bulb we've been ignoring for the last week. It's really important that we go out and buy a replacement. But let's be honest here. No, it isn't. Our mind is playing tricks on us to find alternatives to writing right now.

How do we reduce our desire to avoid writing?

What is really happening is that our desire to write is not sufficient to overcome the effort involved in writing. This is simply a symptom of the

Work Equation going against us. Now we could increase our desire to write. I talked about that back in chapter 3. But there is a limit to how much motivation we can generate — or absorb. At some point, we need to reduce our need for desire to write.

The simplest answer is to make it easier to write, make it fun to write. It's not a job ... it's a game.

Start by making it easier ...

I've already talked about that. Chapters 4, 5, 6, and 7 are all about making writing as effortless as possible. After all, that's why having a good system is so important.

In many cases, finding your motivation and creating your system is enough to make avoidance disappear.

But sometimes, it isn't productive to work so hard, to push your body and mind to the limit. When your productivity falls, the intelligent thing is to take a break. Sometimes a long break — I often need a week or two doing something else after a marathon writing session (e.g. 100 articles in 100 days. Well, I've got to be honest I usually do between 200 and 300 articles in that time frame.

But I'm pretty well burned out by the end of one of these marathons in any case).

In these cases, avoidance is simply your brain telling you it's time to cool it. Time to recharge and get your head together for the next marathon. The real trick then is to take your break but limit it. Only take the time you need and no more.

Short and controlled avoidance is not a big problem. As long as it really is short, controlled, and intentional.

However, frequent and lengthy avoidance behaviors almost always have something behind them (a "hidden agenda"). To eliminate those behaviors, you must discover what is *really* causing the avoidance. Then you can tackle the underlying issue. Maybe you don't want to be successful. Maybe you feel you are faking it. Maybe you want the laurels but not the effort to achieve them. Whatever your issues, you need to identify and resolve them. If you leave the issue unresolved, the avoidance behavior will reoccur. However, when the issue is resolved, avoidance behaviors usually evaporate. At the very least, you may end up redirecting your path through life in a more suitable direction.

Eliminate the time gobblers

Welcome to modern life. It always seems to happen that, whenever we have set aside a chunk of time for writing, we are suddenly in demand from everybody. As Steve Miller said in his song Fly Like An Eagle, "time keeps slipping, slipping ... into the future".

Making our writing easier and faster, and building our desire to write is important. But without the conditions to write, there is little point. And one of those conditions is that we have the time to concentrate. We need to eliminate unnecessary distractions.

Our society has become obsessed with the immediate response. The buzz must be answered. The tweet must be read — even when it's just spam. React, react, react.

Concentrate? Focus? Not so much.

It used to be that the only things that a writer needed to worry about disturbing his or her concentration was the phone, the family, or the bill collector knocking on the door. All that has changed. In order to concentrate on writing, you need to remove yourself from all external communications: phone, email, & personal callers.

Writer's Block Demolition

All those niggly, little warnings that something is happening will decimate your ability to focus.

The first thing you need to do is turn off your email. Especially if you normally use a buzzer or if it flashes up on the screen. The interruption while you are working on the same machine will kill your ability to concentrate. Even worse is that it is occurring on your actual workspace. You are focused on the screen in front of you. If something pops up on it, your focus will automatically change to the movement.

The same thing applies if you use Skype and have it set to alert you when your contacts come online. You can turn the alerts off. By selecting Tools>Options>Notifications you will find a screen that allows you to turn the notifications on and off. Better still, change your status to offline. If you've turned on the facility, Skype will answer and record your calls. You can then deal with them when you've finished writing.

If you use a Twitter client that warns you when a tweet comes in, turn it off. Or if you have a Twitter tool that displays your incoming tweets at the edge of your computer screen, turn it off. In fact, anything that you have which connects you to the outside world needs to be turned off including IM and news feeds.

Of course, the old standby, the phone, is still a source of interruption. Let the answering machine take your calls. Turn off the ringer. Or at least turn it down. Cover the phone with a pillow if you have to. Your phone's ringer is designed to irritate. Believe it or not, the irritation was intentional. You need to prevent that irritation from disrupting your writing.

However, the traditional landline isn't the only phone around now. Don't forget to turn off your cell phone. Especially if you have a smartphone with Twitter alerts and Email alerts and game update alerts and ... well, you get the picture. Turn it off. Let the answering machine handle it. The chances of it being something more important than your writing, and urgent is very, very slim.

And don't forget to close your office door! Make sure your family is aware that you are busy working. You are not to be disturbed unless the house is burning down. A door is also useful for blocking out the unintentional noises, like music or laughter. Remember that a few hours of isolation will be rewarded later.

Of course, not all interruptions are external.

Make sure you have everything at hand. I talked about having a writing hole and writing rituals. This is why. The less time you spend gathering your tools, the less likely the gathering of those tools will become a method of avoiding writing. What you want is to make the decision to write, then to sit down, then to write in the least possible amount of time. And with the least amount of delay. No wasting time looking for things. No wasting time pulling out books or turning on computers or making coffee or whatever other way you can figure out to avoid work. No excuse for not just sitting and working.

You'll often find the advice to do your writing first thing in the morning before you do anything else. This seems to fly in the face of circadian rhythms and working when you are best able to produce. The reason that advice works is simply a variation on the interruption by yourself theme. If you start working on other tasks, they become an excuse to delay working. Starting first thing ensures that you don't substitute "busy work" for writing. So does being disciplined about your writing.

Similarly, breaks during your writing can be a form of delay. Although your overall productivity will be improved by scheduled breaks, unscheduled breaks are a productivity killer. Rather than break off your writing to go the washroom, grab a coffee (or tea) or a sandwich, schedule your breaks. Every forty-five minutes schedule a fifteen-minute break. Go to the washroom at the break, and then grab a coffee and a snack. Another alternative is to schedule the break at the completion of a chapter. This has the advantage of not disturbing the flow of your work. However, the breaks will not be consistent. As a result, you won't train your body to perform necessary functions at the specific times you are scheduled for taking a break.

Get around conflicts

Now you're as efficient as you can be. You're motivated. You're ready and willing to write. You've eliminated the time wasters.

All you need is the actual time...

And that's where modern life tries to mess you up for the last time. It's the last chance that life has and it always seems to know this is the last chance. And it's going to shake you in its jaws until you succumb.

Now, chances are that this actually won't be a problem. If you are sufficiently motivated, no longer avoiding writing, and if writing is easy for you, chances are that you will simply find the time. You'll surf your clock and your calendar and just slide your writing in between the trips to the doctor and dropping the kids at school and all the other little time gobblers. It's strange how we always seem to find the time to watch television or do something that is important to us.

But just in case you really are having trouble finding the spare hour or so a week to dedicate to your book, here are some hints.

Schedule your writing time.

If you don't block out a section of time for an action and then live within that schedule, you won't do the action. That's just the way most of us are. Instead, we'll find something else to do even if it's only resting our eyes. Scheduling a part of your day for writing — and only for writing — can provide the discipline necessary to tip you from never actually getting it done to actually writing and finishing your book.

But do it officially. Place it on your calendar and tell everyone that the time is blocked for working on your book.

Once you've scheduled a block of time for your writing, do not — on pain of failure — ever, ever allow someone to steal your writing time. We've all experienced the "gotta change the plan" event. I'm going to write from nine to ten every morning this week but the wife just made an appointment for the doctor at nine on Thursday and with the chiropractor at 10:15 on Wednesday. And then there is the school interview on Friday at 9:00 ... And on Saturday, I look back at the week that flew by and the book that didn't get written.

You need to block the time and truly reserve it. And you need to make sure your family — and anyone else who controls your calendar — knows that time is already blocked out. That time is yours — it is your future. Use your motivation to justify blocking out the time, if you have to. It's like a doctor's appointment. If you miss the appointment, it's going to cost you twice the cost to make it up. Your writing time is WORK TIME — make sure everyone realizes you are working not playing. No matter how much you enjoy your work.

Schedule your day

One of the tricks that busy executives use is to plan their day. Most of us plan our appointments. At best, we might plan our weeks. Monday at 9:15, I need to go to the doctor's. Wednesday we're going to the school play. Saturday is the ball game. And so on.

However, for many busy executives, the last thing they do at night is to sit down and plan their activities for the next day. From eight to ten I'm going to work on the new strategy. From 10:15 to 11:15 is the appointment with the auditors. From 11:15 to noon, I'm going to wander over to the marketing department and talk with the secretaries. At 12:00, I need to leave for my 12:30 lunch with a client.

This micromanaging of their day allows them to focus on a specific task for a specific length of time. It's the only way they can be sure to accomplish everything that they need to accomplish in an overloaded day. It also requires them to prioritize their activities and avoid wasting time on unimportant actions.

Scheduling your day can help you to find extra time to accomplish your writing. Simply identify what is important to accomplish, assign a time for any previously scheduled times, and then slot in a time for each of the other tasks you need to accomplish. Create the next day's schedule the last thing at night, every night. If you break the routine, you will eventually stop scheduling your day. And you'll find your day filling up with nonsense once again.

Three strategies for stealing time

With the last two hints — scheduling writing time and scheduling your day — I've focused on becoming more effective in the use of time. I've eliminated the time spent on less important tasks. And I've used a disciplined approach to ensure that time is spent only on what is important — which includes writing a book.

Unfortunately, sometimes that just isn't enough.

One of the realities of modern life is that we often find ourselves trying to squeeze too many activities into too little time. We become flustered and frantic. If we want to write, we are going to need to steal time from other tasks.

Use Saturday or Sunday mornings

Most of us have one day a week where we don't schedule anything. You need it for sanity. It's a day where you recharge your batteries. A day to recover from the frantic schedule of your week. Maybe you run around doing chores that you can't get done otherwise. Or maybe you sleep in that day. Maybe you just relax and spend it with the family. Often you hide the fact this is a day off by scheduling family events such as picnics or visits to a museum or shopping.

Pick that day and steal it for writing (don't forget to schedule it). You can't steal all of it without hurting your family and yourself. However, squeezing an hour or two for your writing can be as cathartic as any other form of relaxation you use the day for. And on that day, we usually waste as much time as we use. So squeezing an hour in for writing isn't as much of a burden as you might imagine.

Smart multitasking.

If you check the want ads, one of the more common phrases is "able to multitask". References to multitasking are part of the popular culture. They are everywhere.

There's only one problem.

We can't multitask ... it's a myth. Our brains can't handle it. In order to fake multitasking what we do is stop and quickly shift focus, then stop and shift focus back again. Unfortunately, every time we stop we lose part of the efficiency of our efforts. That's why you need to eliminate interruptions while you work.

However, there are many cases where we are wasting time while we do some task or other. Situations where our focus doesn't need to be on the task at hand. Situations where we can be doing something else.

Smart multitasking is simply a matter of making best use of these wasted times.

For example, waiting for a doctor involves sitting in the waiting room (often for hours) and listening for our name to be called. Instead of sitting and reading six-month-old magazines, why not take a tablet and write your book while you wait?

Waiting for laundry is another example of largely wasted time. While your hands are required to fold the laundry or shift from the washing machine to the drier, your mind (and your mouth) can be busy writing your next book. Take a portable, digital recorder with you and write your book for later transcription. Even your smartphone or MP3 player will work. Even if you aren't interested in saving those two or three minutes, take along a laptop, notebook or tablet and write while you are sitting waiting for the machines to finish. The screen is only slightly more difficult to watch than clothes tumbling around behind the glass. And a lot more interesting.

Television is another major time waster. I'm not talking about the quality of the shows or the fact that it's a passive, solitary experience. I'm referring to the fact that 15 minutes per hour are spent in watching commercials. Usually the same commercials. Spending time with your family watching a favorite television show is not wasted time. But use the PVR and time shift it. That time wasted watching the same commercials over and over is far better spent writing and producing something worth reading. Even if you don't have a PVR, use the commercial time to write.

In my case, my wife doesn't drive. She needs me to run her out to the grocery store and for other shopping expeditions. Rather than wander around the store, pushing the cart where she doesn't want to go, and moving it when she wants it to stay in a particular place, I find a local coffee shop. I use that time to write and gain a good hour of writing per week. She calls or text messages me when she finishes and I go pick her up. Everyone is happy and we're both productive.

Always carry a notebook with you ... tablet computers are a great invention. Notebooks are cool too, and much easier to carry than a full sized laptop. If you're desperate or just hate technology, a pad and paper or a journal should be your constant companion.

Even if you can't write during these snatched moments, maybe you can design or research your next book. Many coffee shops and fast food restaurants have free WiFi. For that matter, cell phone data plans are no longer the financial drain they once were.

With a bit of effort on your part, you can easily identify other situations where you are required to be physically present but not mentally present. These are perfect situations to exploit for smart multi-tasking

Add an hour to your day

Sometimes, the only way you are going to get the time to write is if they built a 25-hour day. The only solution in that case is to add an hour to your day. Get up early or go to bed later and use the time gained for your writing.

Chances are your whole family gets up at the same time every day. They fight for the washroom, rush through their breakfast, and rush out to school, or work, or wherever they have to be. This time is hectic, frantic, and confused with everyone trying to use the same facilities at the same time.

So get up an hour or two earlier. You'll be surprised at how much work you can do while the house is quiet. Why do think busy executives tend to go into the office so early? It's not that they can squeeze an extra hour out of the day. It's that the hour they squeeze while no one else is in the office is the most productive hour of their day.

Even if you can't maintain the longer hours every day ... get up early or go to bed later three times a week. After all, the modern condition is sleep deprived and less sleep may not work for you. However, by giving up sleep three times a week, you'll add at least three hours of writing a week and that's a lot better than not writing your book at all.

Writer's Block Demolition

"There is no real ending. It's just the place where you stop the story."
— Frank Herbert

Chapter 9:

Conclusion - Time to Get Started Writing

Finally, I am at the end of the book. I hope that the journey has been interesting and thought provoking for you. And I particularly hope that you have been able to pick up ideas, tips, and techniques that will aid you in your writing endeavors.

Just to repeat one more time (well, maybe *two* times) what we've said throughout these nine chapters...

Finding time to write needs you to focus on three elements. Find what motivates you and then make sure your writing and it are closely linked. Put out signs and make sure you know why you are writing. Make sure your work habits, rituals and

Writer's Block Demolition

system helps you to write — otherwise they will hinder your writing! Writing has to be easy to do or you will avoid it! And finally, you've got to clear time in your schedule and then force yourself to own that time as your writing time.

Avoiding writer's block requires you to focus on two of those elements — motivation and your system. Your system must guide you through the thoughts you are writing about. The motivation will then carry you through. After that, it's just the occasional (very occasional) need for you to think outside the box that may result in writer's block.

Writer's block and finding the time to write are both symptoms of the same problems. They have the same solutions. Finding the time to write automatically solves the writer's block problem. Solving writer's block requires you to solve any problems you might have with finding the time to write.

To put it another way:

- Eliminate the fear of writing
- Build your desire to write until it fills your soul
- Lose your bad habits.

and suddenly the time and your writing will both magically appear.

Good luck with your book. Get out your computer, find the time to write and destroy that (mythical) "writer's block"!

For more information on this and related topics visit our blog at

http://www.LearningCreators.com.

About the Author:
Glen Ford

Glen Ford is a co-founder and Chief Operating Officer with VProz Inc. He is a serial entrepreneur having set up the internet training company TrainingNOW and its subsidiaries as well as providing consulting services for startups in Debt Counseling, Software and Payment Processing. He has been principal of his own project management consultancy for over 11 years. During that time he has alternated his clients between government, the big banks and small to medium companies. Prior to that he spent 10 years working for the Canadian Standards Association and 10 years alternating between large distribution and manufacturing companies. Prior to that he worked for a very successful HVAC firm.

Glen is active in the business community as a member of The Project Management Institute (PMI) Lakeshore Chapter and a former training director for BNI Eagles Chapter of Business Network International (BNI). Glen is also an active supporter of charity including Scouts Canada (3rd Erin Mills Scouts). Glen holds a BSc from McMaster University in Hamilton, an MCPM from York University (Schulich), and a PMP (Project Management Professional) designation.

Glen has been involved in the internet since 1995. He has been blogging since before content management systems such as WordPress existed.

TrainingNOW

TrainingNOW is a training and publishing company located in Mississauga and Burlington, Ontario, Canada. It provides specialized web hosting services for companies seeking to deliver "how to" education over the web. It also publishes and sells "how to" books and training materials in digital, print and other media. Through its subsidiaries LearningCreators and ContentCreators it provides custom training material development. TrainingNOW maintains the following websites to provide specific training:

http://www.LearningCreators.com provides training in learning content product creation (webinars, podcasts, books and eBooks).

http://www.HowDoYouBlog.biz
http://www.HowToBlogMoney.com
and http://www.HowToBlogCourse.com provide training on various aspects of writing and monetizing blogs.

TrainingNOW Books By Glen Ford

How to Write Your Own How-To EBook in 24 Hours or Less: The Information Products Secret Revealed!

How to Document a Project Plan: What You Need To Know To Design A Project Management Plan Quickly and Easily

How to Blog for Money: 9 Strategies to Get Your Blog Earning Money Online and Off

As Glen Douglas

How To Build A Raised Garden Bed

With Paul Benson

101 Limericks About Public Speaking

www.ingramcontent.com/pod-product-compliance
Lightning Source LLC
Chambersburg PA
CBHW071845230426
43671CB00012B/2076